ENTREPRENEURSHIP
AND THE
CORPORATION

ENTREPRENEURSHIP AND THE CORPORATION

WILLIAM COPULSKY

HERBERT W. McNULTY

amacom

A DIVISION OF AMERICAN MANAGEMENT ASSOCIATIONS

International standard book number: 0-8144-5348-1

Library of Congress catalog card number: 73-85191

FIRST PRINTING

PREFACE

THIS is a book about entrepreneurship and the large corporation. Entrepreneurship is the spark of small company operation that can help large companies to be more effective in certain areas, especially new ventures, and to improve results in all areas. But it is more. The dinosaur's doom was sealed when it became too large and too unwieldy—and failed to adapt to changes in its environment. As today's corporations become larger and larger, and as the rate of change in the environment accelerates, the options that remain to corporations may dwindle to a choice between adaptation and extinction. Present indications are that entrepreneurship can be a notably successful adaptive route for the large corporation that chooses not to walk in the footsteps of the dinosaur.

These pages reflect extensive experience and extensive reading, but the opinions they contain are our own and do not necessarily reflect those of the companies or organizations we are or have been affiliated with.

The text is salted with little illustrative stories about Harry A. and Phil C. and others. All are figments of our imagination and have no living counterparts. We hope this will save the reader the trouble of trying to figure out who they really are and leave him free to enjoy our fictions.

WILLIAM COPULSKY
HERBERT W. McNULTY

CONTENTS

vii

CHAPTER 1

WHY ENTREPRENEURSHIP IN THE CORPORATION?

GERALD B. Zornow, chairman of the board of Eastman Kodak, has described the introduction of entrepreneurship into the corporation as in the nature of "asking an elephant to ice-skate." What is meant by entrepreneurship? Is its lack a deficiency of the large company? Is it a necessity? To answer these questions, a definition of terms is necessary.

From the viewpoint of the economist, there are four factors of production: capital, land, labor, and enterprise. The function of enterprise is to combine and manage the other three factors in such a way as to produce a profit. Profit is the return on enterprise, as interest is on capital, rent on land, and wages on labor. When the world of business was small and underdeveloped, the institutional factors of production could be easily identified with the person who performed the functions of the factor: rent with the landlord, for example, and enterprise with the entrepreneur.

The word *entrepreneur* comes from the French *entreprendre*—to undertake. Thus an entrepreneur is a person who undertakes to organize, manage, and assume the risk of a business. This is a large risk, and the entrepreneur who fails becomes an undertaker in another sense. Because in large busi-

1

ness the function of enterprise is borne by many rather than by one, and is not, as a rule, centralized in a single person, entrepreneurs are usually associated with small business. In fact, an entrepreneur is often defined as the owner of a small business, who performs all or most of the business functions himself.

Large companies and small companies are run in different ways to match their differing needs. When companies become large they give up some of the sensitivity, flexibility, and responsiveness they had when they were small. Yet these are virtues that can contribute to large company success, especially in such areas as new ventures. The lack of flexibility in large companies poses a special problem when they acquire small businesses. What is to be done with the entrepreneur-owners? Should they be retained or retired? If the company favors keeping them on, can they be motivated to stay?

The study of the role of entrepreneurship in the large company is made difficult by a screen of public relations verbiage that hides the actualities. For the most part the efforts to introduce entrepreneurship are undertaken prematurely, announced with great fanfare, and buried quietly when they fail. And fail they do, because adequate conceptual thinking is rare.

The Pros and Cons of Entrepreneurship   Advocates of increased entrepreneurship in the corporation are convinced that simulation of the small business environment will overcome the limitations of large company management. In their view, this is of especial importance in new ventures, which start out as small businesses. They see large corporations with their established procedures as strangulating the innovative impulse and quenching the enthusiasm of the newcomer. This is because the tendency is to have corporate staff members evaluate each proposed new venture, and they find it easier and less risky to say no than yes. Yet new projects need champions not no-men. When entrepreneurial companies are acquired, their former owners are likely to find the corporation's thumbs-down approach to their creative ideas so stifling that they walk out and leave the acquisition as a problem to the acquirer.

The traditional large company has a vertical organization with several management layers, which slows decision making. At the same time, its personnel find few opportunities for self-development and job satisfaction where jobs are specialized and responsibility and authority are limited.

Now the business environment is changing, and the traditional corporation is faced with three critical problems that can no longer be brushed aside:

1. Overcoming the increasing difficulty of launching new ventures and commercializing research
2. Keeping acquired entrepreneurs and their businesses growing and profitable
3. Giving hope for self-development and job satisfaction to unhappy management personnel who are aggressive or ambitious

Perhaps adaptation is not the answer. Perhaps businesses are large or small by nature, and they venture into each other's areas of competence only at their own risk—a very substantial risk.

As contrasted with the advocates of entrepreneurship, the opponents see more problems than profits. The entrepreneurial personality, they tell us, is not easily fitted into the corporate structure. Why should corporate orderliness be upset by entrepreneurship? Orderliness is characteristic of, and needed by, many large organizations: business, the military, the church, the state. A change in organization may be a simplistic and harmful response to deep problems. Only to the naïve does change alone appear to be a benefit. In the days of Nero, Petronius wrote perceptively about this:

We trained hard, but it seemed that every time we were beginning to form up into teams we would be reorganized. I was to learn later in life that we tend to meet any new situation by reorganizing, and a wonderful method it can be for creating the illusion of progress while producing confusion, inefficiency and demoralization.

Entrepreneurship Here and Abroad   In respect to entrepreneurship and its role in large corporations, U.S. firms are considerably ahead of firms in other countries in both problems and solutions. Some thought has been given to these problems in other countries, but little action has been taken. This may be attributable at least in part to substantial differences between the goals and objectives of businessmen in different countries. One difference is in attitudes toward profits. In America, profit is a primary criterion; in Japan, businessmen pay heed to the national interest as well. Another difference is in personal authority. Decentralization is common in the United States but uncommon abroad. And in America job-hopping is routine, whereas in Europe and Japan, companies and employees are committed to each other.

In Britain, executive promotion is linked to social class and education in the right school. Higher education still is not the norm. Less than half of all executives are university graduates—but the chances are that the man who is not a graduate wears the right school tie. Most British executives believe there is no way to train managers, much less entrepreneurs.

Japanese employees are likely to work for the same company throughout their careers, from the time they come out of school to the time when they retire at age 55. Compensation depends on the length of service. The Japanese company and its employees are like a close family. From the viewpoint of the employee, his future and his family's future depend on the success of the company that employs him. If the company does well, so does he; if the company does badly, so does he. Thus, because personal and company success are irrevocably intermeshed, the employee's motivation to work hard and do well by his employer is strong.

But conditions are changing outside the United States just as they are here, and as they come to match American conditions, we can expect the problems to match as well. Katsuji Kawamata, president of Nissan Motor Company, has recently pointed out that increasing education and income, together with changes in family structure, have led to problems.[1] Younger Japanese employees, for example, are voicing a strong sense of doubt as to the meaningfulness of assigned work.

BIG BUSINESS AND SMALL BUSINESS

No one would be so foolhardy as to insist that big business and small business can be run in the same way. The two differ in needs as well as in objectives. But both can benefit from interaction and understanding.

Aims and Goals of Big Business   Big business can be characterized by the term *managerial enterprise*. This is a system of production and distribution, unified by policies and controlled by managers whose aim is to administer the business in such a way as to insure continuity.

The managers are not owners. The owners are stockholders, and their interests are, at least in theory, represented in the company by a board of directors. The stockholders may have little concern about the company and its operations except

[1] "Work Ethic Weakening Under Impact of Increased Education and Leisure, Says Head of Nissan Motors," *Japan Economic Report* (April 1, 1973).

as they affect the stock price, but the managers who operate the company have other goals as well. Of course, rises in stock price are important to managers, especially those who have stock options. But other forms of compensation and other incentives are motivating forces to managers, perhaps the most important being the good health of the enterprise which supports them.

As outlined by Oswald Knauth, the distinctive features of managerial enterprise are

- A large capital investment of maximum efficiency for a single purpose
- Action based on policies formulated to strengthen the business
- Creation of demand constant enough to permit planned production at predetermined prices
- Separation of ownership and management
- Ability to increase production at lower costs
- Continuity of operation

The primary concern of managerial enterprise is to survive; the secondary concern is to strengthen its trade position. Its actions are primarily governed by long-range policies rather than opportunism and profit maximization. Overhead expenses are high. Companies try to control the market, but control is always limited and temporary. Yet they survive this, just as they survive technical, economic, social, and political changes.

Competition is not by price alone, and success is contingent on goodwill, repetitive demand, and increasing efficiency in serving an ever widening group of customers.

Because there must be steady demand, businessmen strive for a reputation that will attract and hold customers, an assured source of raw materials, good trade connections, and access to complete research, legal, and other services. The number and importance of trade advantages determine the degree of control exercised over the market in achieving steadiness of demand and volume (but not price).

In classical economic theory of free enterprise, scarcity of goods is presupposed. As demand increases, according to this view, marginal resources and methods are used. This results in higher costs, which in turn make prices rise until demand levels off and a new equilibrium is reached at higher prices.

But from the managerial enterprise viewpoint there is an almost unlimited ability to produce at decreasing costs, which brings increasing demand, which in turn brings increased output at lower costs, which further stimulates demand. Here market and laboratory research services are needed to find new uses for products and convert luxuries into necessities.

The function of management in manufacturing industries is to synchronize the steady flow of raw materials to men and equipment and then to a maintained market. There are nine essential operations in this process:

1. Keeping the records of the business
2. Obeying the laws
3. Raising money
4. Providing for technical development
5. Conforming to consumer demand
6. Cultivating and keeping a good reputation
7. Strengthening competitive advantages and industry position
8. Setting price policies
9. Handling relations with governments

Managers set goals that incorporate budgets, standards, and quotas, all of which are carefully watched and studied.

Some trade advantages accrue in the ordinary course of business, others have to be won. It is up to management to improve every trade position and guard against mischance. Almost all trade advantages can be duplicated, given enough time, money, and ingenuity. Some—patents, for example, and ownership of raw materials—are more difficult to duplicate than others. If the holder of a trade advantage tries to exploit it by charging excessive prices or by offering products of poor quality, he may destroy the advantage he has worked so hard to establish. The fundamental trade advantage is reputation built on (1) guaranty of satisfaction, (2) service, (3) prestige.

Under managerial enterprise, costs are determined by long-range considerations such as depreciation, financing, and research programs. Prices are administered by policies that are set after the determining factors have been surveyed. The main factor in setting price is long-term stability, in a dynamic sense that allows for declining price as there is increasing demand. Price policies are variously designed to achieve stability, capture expanding markets, lower cost during depressed business periods, and meet or forestall competition. Price policies are rarely designed to maximize profits. In fact, no one is even quite sure how to measure profits or costs, especially within a definite time period.

Aims and Goals of Small Business   In contrast, the owner of a small business has all he can do to survive. He must scratch and scramble for enough business to keep him going tomorrow, next month, next year. He is the owner, the manager—everything. With little reputation, he has to compete by offering his product at a lower price. He cannot control the market or his environment. He has constant battles with suppliers and customers. He has no staff services or support. He is reluctant to put out the money for accounting and legal services. When he consults with his market research department he is talking to himself. He has no long-term budgets, no quotas, no reserves. If he shows a profit, he's happy; if he doesn't, he's out of business.

Carl Pacifico, who has been a key executive in a highly successful small company, recently pointed out some of the myths of small business.[2] Small company entrepreneurs have many problems and are well aware of them, though outsiders are not. The outstanding performance of a few small companies is not typical, and most small companies stay small. Moreover, larger companies tend to make a higher percentage of returns on assets than small companies. If taxable profit is siphoned off into expenses, the larceny is minor; the combined salaries plus expenses paid to owners and officers of small companies tend to be far less than salaries in large companies. The small company owner has to wait until he can sell out to make any sizable fortune—if he can sell out profitably. And the capacity to absorb losses is limited in a small company. It lacks the resources to carry it through lean periods, and a short run of bad management will destroy it. In a large company the manager has a great deal of information and expertise at his disposal, but in a small company the manager has to rely on intuition as a substitute for internal specialists or consultants.

Yet small business is not dead. According to Census Bureau 1967 figures, 22 percent of nonagricultural U.S. employment is in companies with fewer than 20 employees. In manufacturing, only 5 percent of employees are in these smaller firms, so it is apparent that small businesses are much more common in the service industries.

The president of a large American manufacturing corporation asks: "Why is it that a little company without the advan-

[2] "The Small Company Mystique," paper presented at Division of Chemical Marketing and Economics, American Chemical Society. Dallas, Tex., April 10, 1973.

tages of professionalism, established research programs, lots of cash, and a surplus of management can beat the large corporation on benefits versus costs?" There are some legitimate answers to such a question:

1. *Wrong objective.* The large corporation may be mistakenly concentrating on growth as a goal and ignoring limits. At some point the antitrust laws come into play and limit growth or the direction of growth.

2. *Lack of new directions.* Large companies find it easier to expand their current lines than to go off in new directions.

3. *Oversophistication.* Large companies tend to oversophisticated analysis of new projects.

Basically, the large company is limited by its need to keep the long run in mind. If the small company fails it will close up, and its way is to stay with a project until it succeeds or goes bankrupt. The large company will carry a product until its computerized discounted flow analysis says to quit.

Limitations of Big and Small Businesses   Both big and small businesses have serious limitations related to the systems under which they operate. Big business doesn't respond easily to change. Its orientation is to the long term rather than the short term. Once the system is established and functioning smoothly, only small evolutionary changes can be easily assimilated into the system. Large revolutionary changes are disruptive, and their effect is unpredictable. Because of this, the very controls designed for ordered efficiency can be the death blow to a new venture. Urgent day-to-day problems—putting out fires—take management attention, and new projects wait on the shelf.

What small business lacks is standing and reputation. This is why a new small business in the shelter of a large company has immense advantages over the independent small business. Knauth has said, about reputation:

The indispensability of reputation is most evident when it is lacking. All transactions become difficult and cumbersome. Every new product starts from scratch. It seems to take twice as long and cost twice as much as anyone ever thought to launch a new product. Quality must be proven and performance demonstrated. New products show defects in use. When corrected, persuading consumers is a long, hard job.[3]

Building trade connections may entail many years of profitable and pleasant dealings before orders are placed over the phone with confidence. Will the quality of goods be up to standard? The price right? Delivery punctual? Turning occasional customers into regular customers is hard work, as is finding new customers. In the meantime, costs are high until the many money-saving tricks of the trade are learned.

Small companies hit a critical phase when their sales reach a range in the order of $5 million to $15 million a year. There are several reasons for this:

1. The entrepreneurial manager generally is naïve as to the need for decentralization and continues a one-man show beyond the limit of effective one-man management.

2. The time required to develop a solid business exceeds five years, during which period the product or service matures to a point where large additional investments are required.

3. New products have to be developed to supplement the original successful product before the company is large enough to bear this substantial cost without undue effect on the overall picture. Furthermore, there is usually a limit to the initial specialty markets. Large sales require broad markets, which in turn require heavy investment and attract strong competition.

Initially, the small company relies on the specific marketing or technical skill of the founder and entrepreneur. When sales grow to the $5 million to $15 million a year range, financial and organization skills become critical. Past $15 million in

[3] Oswald Knauth, *Managerial Enterprise*. New York: W. W. Norton (1948), p. 81.

annual sales, companies need more products and run into more competition; thus marketing skills become critical.

At many critical points small companies have limited alternatives: stay small, get big, or be acquired by a large company. It is when they choose to be acquired that they create a different kind of problem for the acquirer: how to keep the entrepreneurial spirit viable and growing.

Profits Versus Stock Price   It was pointed out that large companies concentrate on the long term and do not attempt to optimize short-term profits. Moreover, in the large company it is often difficult to measure profits; they are sometimes viewed as a means of affecting stock price, not a means of measuring results. Even when a measure of total profits is available, it is difficult to measure the contribution of individuals to profits. Yet profit results are the motive force of entrepreneurs. Unless they have quick, quantitative feedback on the results of their actions they tend to be unhappy.

In the large public company, profit targets become confused with stock price targets. Profits are what interest entrepreneurs; the price per share is what interests stockholders. Profit is only one of several factors that affect stock price. To clarify this, let us consider two questions: (1) What are profits? (2) How do profits enter into stock price determination?

The entrepreneur tends to consider profits as arising from manufacturing and trading operations. In classical economic theory, the function of the entrepreneur is to combine the other factors of production (capital, land, and labor) to produce a profit (the reward to the enterprise factor). However, from the viewpoint of financially oriented, large company management, profit is only one factor in determining earnings per share. And it is earnings per share that is one of the main factors in determining stock price—the figure that is the focus of stockholder attention.

The following are some of the factors which will tend to increase a company's earnings per share:

1. Use of borrowed capital.
2. Acquisition of companies whose price-earnings ratio is lower than that of the acquiring company.
3. Deferring of certain expenses, such as research and development, which can be capitalized.

Figure 1 shows some of the confused relationships between profits and stock price.

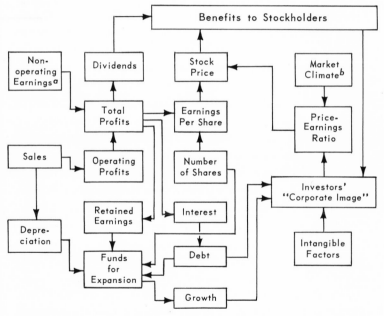

[a] Nonoperating earnings include capital gains as well as the effect of leverage through favorable acquisitions.

[b] Market climate includes such factors as the outlook for the industry the company is in, the outlook for the stock market overall as measured by the Dow-Jones or similar market index, and the economic and monetary factors which affect these outlooks.

Figure 1. Relationship between profits and stock prices.

The earnings per share criterion confuses operating decisions with financial policies. However, since it is derived from a combination of operating and financial considerations, it may be an appropriate goal for the large corporation which aims to benefit stockholders. It can be argued that in the long run the goal of maximizing share price rather than operating profits is most appropriate for large public corporations. This is because the share price is looked on as a long-term measure of the expected future performance of the large company, taking into account both financial and operating skills. A merger or a particular financial structure will tend to increase share price only if shareholders perceive it as contributing to future earnings per share. Unfortunately, many other factors affect share price in the short run. This makes short-term investing in the stock market a psychological game in which the trick is to spot next week's fad before anyone else does.

The entrepreneur is unmoved by this. He is interested in the results of his own efforts and is motivated by a goal stated in terms of operating profits. It merely confuses him to be told that he must worry about financial policies and earnings per share, which he considers top management's task. Unless this is made clear at the operating levels, the entrepreneurial spirit will be dampened.

ENTREPRENEURSHIP IN THE CORPORATE ENVIRONMENT

Perhaps Gerald Zornow was right when he said that introducing entrepreneurship into the corporate environment may be something like teaching an elephant to ice-skate. Entrepreneurs tend to have personalities antagonistic to the corporate climate, and their socioeconomic and educational backgrounds are likely to be radically different from those of corporate executives. Yet the greatest problem is not in learning to live with the entrepreneur but in finding him and bringing him on board.

Psychological tests are helpful in screening out those who do not have the makings of an entrepreneur, but they are of little use in identifying the few who do have the qualities of entrepreneurship. Corporate management often mislabels or misidentifies entrepreneurs. Hiring, screening, and training are carried out by management development or personnel departments with no operating experience. They set up organizational problems that obstruct rather than encourage entrepreneurship, and they lean toward the Harvard M.B.A., the staff man, the Ivy Leaguer, the ambitious, aggressive young conformist. On the other side of the coin, when entrepreneurs are hired they are likely to wind up in jobs that stifle them and make them unhappy and ineffective.

A number of business practices discourage entrepreneurship:

- Key decision making centralized in top management
- Unwillingness to take a long pay-out period for a new venture
- Inflexible organization
- Discouragement of risk taking
- Hiring practices that favor conformity and weed out potential entrepreneurs
- Insistence that new ventures bear a so-called fair share of corporate overhead

An entrepreneur who owned his own business would beg, borrow or find some other way to keep his overhead and extra services to a minimum. In a large corporation he has easy access to and is expected to use the corporation's resources. These resources are one of the supposed advantages of being in a large company. But the entrepreneur may be penalized for using them because assessments and allocated charges are unduly burdensome. Yet the changing corporate environment and the growth in corporate size may make a solution for these problems essential to corporate survival. The dinosaur was too big for a changing environment. It didn't adapt, and it didn't survive. Can the large corporation escape its fate?

WHAT MAKES THE ENTREPRENEUR TICK

Entrepreneurship is linked with authority, with responsibility, and with the satisfaction of the entrepreneur's desire to achieve goals which motivate him. These needs loom ever larger as a factor in the corporation's own fundamental need for survival.

Abraham Maslow, late chairman of the psychology department of Brandeis University, postulated a hierarchy of needs ranging from the most fundamental needs to insure survival to the highest needs for fulfillment of the intellect and the spirit. As needs change, so do motivations. One way of forecasting changes in motivation is to trace a man's movement up the progression of needs in the hierarchy. Taking the needs in the hierarchy in order from lowest to highest:

1. *Physiological needs.* To survive, a man must have food, clothing, and shelter. These are his most basic needs because without them he cannot stay alive.

2. *Safety or security needs.* Once his survival needs are satisfied, our man turns his attention to safeguarding himself against danger, threats, and losses. Now survival is no longer a motivator; stabilizing his environment for the future is the dominant issue.

3. *Social needs.* When survival and security are assured, a man wants to reach outside himself and become part of a larger society. He wants to belong, to share, to have friends, to love. The approval of the people around him is now the dominant motivator in his life.

4. *Ego needs.* With his social needs satisfied, a man turns to the need to improve his self-esteem and win the esteem of others. He wants self-confidence, knowledge, independence, a sense of achievement, a sense of competence. He also wants to be recognized by others—with status, appreciation, respect. Money becomes important, not only because it measures achievement but because it can buy the status symbols with which one's achievement can be exhibited to others.

5. *Self-fulfillment needs.* This is the highest level in the hierarchy. Man wants to realize his full individual potential as a human being. He wants to grow, to develop himself. Maslow calls this step self-actualization.

At each level of the hierarchy, needs determine values, patterns of behavior, and motivation. For example, at the survival level, man values food, clothing, shelter, and other basic needs most highly. But once a need is satisfied, it is no longer a motivator of behavior. When we are not hungry we will not bestir ourselves to acquire food. Now higher-level needs come into play, in an approximation of the sequence in the hierarchy. (In some of us, for example, the need for esteem may come before any social needs.)

The pattern of movement along the hierarchy is up, but when a lower-level need is no longer met, a man slides down the scale to the lower level. If he loses the job that earns him the money to buy food and shelter, he will ignore his social and ego needs until his physiological and security needs are satisfied once again.

Although Maslow's hierarchy of values is based on observation, but never proved, experience seems to support the hypothesis for individuals and for nations. Large parts of the world are still at the survival and security levels. But in the United States the bulk of the vast middle class is operating on the basis of social and ego needs, and many have set their sights on developing their own capabilities for their own satisfaction.

Maslow called the first four needs deficit needs, because in each case the motivation is to overcome a lack of something: food, safety, love, esteem. The fifth—self-fulfillment or self-actualization—is called a growth need. The person who reaches this point is eager to realize his potential. The self-actualized person is spontaneous, creative, and capable of deriving immense satisfaction from his achievements.

Because each person is unique, the form or content of self-actualization is highly individual and the satisfactions are almost entirely internal. A self-actualizing artist is motivated to paint and derives gratification from the act of painting rather than the finished product.

There is much evidence that for many managers who have moved up the hierarchy and satisfied their ego needs, their need for self-fulfillment can be satisfied through entrepreneurship. Without some method of self-fulfillment, tensions and dissatisfaction can lead to lower performance levels. If Maslow's needs hierarchy is correct, relentless pressure will force corporate managements to a critical stage unless self-achievement needs can be served.

The Youthful Entrepreneur   Many businessmen have misinterpreted the actions and attitudes of young people toward business. Older businessmen talk about the antibusiness attitude of youth, of a desire to avoid responsibility and to avoid work.

Yet the contrary is true. The willingness to work and the willingness to accept authority and responsibility are there; the problem is to channel motivations and attitudes which already exist in the culture and the individual. Our instinct disposes us to favor productive efficiency and deprecate waste. This instinct, said the economist Thorstein Veblen, "asserts itself even under very adverse circumstances." If college students reject the chance to fit snugly into a slot in big corporations with a good title and a good salary, it is not because they abhor business, but because their value and reward system has progressed beyond social group and ego needs. Their need is for self-fulfillment, which status and salary alone will not satisfy as long as the individual potential is limited.

Michael Fontanello, a 1967 graduate of the University of Hartford, worked for six months in a management training program and then left in disgust. Today, his long black hair tied back, wearing jeans and a work shirt, he functions as president of Students of Berkeley, Inc., a collection of non-profit stores which sells records, stereo equipment, and bicycles. He will not work again for a large corporation "even though I sometimes work 10 to 12 hours a day at $3 per hour like everyone else. . . ." A business major at a nearby business college says business is looked down upon by college students "not because it's decadent, but because it's boring."

Deaver Brown, 26 years old, with B.A. and M.B.A. from Harvard, joined forces with Alexandre Goodwin, 25, a lawyer, to launch Cross River Products, which makes collapsible baby strollers and backpacks. After about two years of struggle, the business was doing $4 million a year in sales, paying the two founders $25,000 a year each, showing a respectable profit, and providing employment for 170 besides.

Deaver Brown had been a rising young product manager with General Foods at $25,000 a year. When asked about his attitude toward large companies he said: I was ready to get out. . . . Not that General Foods treated me badly—I think they paid me more than they should have. But it seemed to me that like all big companies, the payoffs had less to do with what I did to help the company than with personal self-promotion. And it was almost impossible to see the results of your work. Here I know, if I make a mistake, whose mistake it is—mine—and the repercussions are direct and fast. It's the same with the right moves.

At General Foods I worked a 35-hour week, I made good money, and I was constantly dissatisfied. Here I work an 80-hour week, I have yet to see good money, and I'm happy.[4]

When Work Is Soulless . . .   Albert Camus has said, "Without work, all life goes rotten. But when work is soulless, life stifles and dies. . . ." Our so-called Puritan ethic, which teaches that work is good and idle hands are the devil's tools, has not disappeared. Americans are not altogether removed from the pioneer society which required hard work for survival or from their immigrant forebears, who worked hard in a new land. The *desire* to work hard has not disappeared; what may be disappearing is the *opportunity* to work hard at rewarding work. One example of the persistence of the desire to work is the way Americans use their leisure time. As leisure time increases, Americans are moving away from passive spectator activities into active participative sports and recreation. Skiing and tennis are booming. Sociologists tell us that a prime reason for the switch to participative sports is a desire to obtain emotional satisfaction from these leisure activities to compensate for the lack of satisfaction on the job. Many people have transformed their play into work or imitations of work because they can set challenging goals for themselves in sports, as the entrepreneur can set and face challenging goals in his own business.

Scott Myers has pointed out that recreation can be a useful model for a satisfactory job. A happy bowler has a visible, challenging, but attainable goal. He sets his own standards. He receives immediate feedback. His successes earn recognition. The fun would go if he couldn't see the pins go down and get his score, if the rules were changed without telling him why, if credit and recognition went only to the team cap-

[4] Barbara Davidson, "Two Guys Who Made It with Their 'Umbroller,'" *New York Times Magazine* (January 7, 1973), pp. 38 ff.

tain, or if he went bowling under threat or to get paid for his time.

Just as we progressed many years ago from an agricultural to an industrial society, we are now in a time of transition from an industrial to a postindustrial society. An *industrial society* is one in which the problems of production have been solved, and the main challenge is to generate enough demand to absorb the capacity of the factories and farms. Increases in growth depend upon expansion of demand, as do employment and income. A *postindustrial society* is one in which people turn their focus from earning and spending to a search for more freedom, more time to develop themselves and improve the quality of their lives. This change may impinge on the industrial-oriented society by causing a loss in productivity as motivation to earn and spend decreases.

We have assumed that all men are "economic" men who want to maximize their real income. But an increasing number want to maximize their life-style, the way in which they spend both work and leisure time. For these people income is balanced against commuting time, work satisfaction, doing one's thing, education, or a second career.

Can the large corporation provide challenge and satisfaction? And if it does, will the corporation benefit? The answer is yes to both questions.

Not everyone will be receptive to the ideas in this book. While business is one of the central activities of our world, it rarely turns inward for genuine self-examination. Business is often anti-intellectual, yet it poses deep intellectual problems to which the generally accepted answers are often not the right answers; in fact, the stated problems may not even be the right problems. Widely held opinions are often based on conditions that no longer exist. The fact is that the management of business is worth the most serious thought. It is not only our youth who are frustrated and cynical; many of those in high places who have long been committed to business careers also have doubts. All can gain fresh insights from realistic thinking and reappraisal.

The current industrial society is about three generations old—not old enough to be well understood or to provide the perspective of history. Yet we are already moving into the postindustrial society. The times when business belonged to an entrepreneur and his family alone are gone. The time when it is run by managers from the top down is going. To an increasing extent, future success will depend on whether employees think of "our business," not "their business." Creating an entrepreneurial atmosphere may thus be the key to survival.

This doesn't mean that we have to recreate the entrepreneurship of the 1800s; that world is gone. We need fewer men who can organize, run, and control a business single-handed. But we do need entrepreneurs who can work in the corporate atmosphere of the twentieth and twenty-first centuries and who are aware, spirited, and able to look beyond the detail to see the totality of a problem and solve it.

CHAPTER 2

THE ENTREPRENEURIAL PERSONALITY

IN ORDER to understand the entrepreneurial personality in the confines of the large corporation and how this personality might be harnessed for the benefit of both entrepreneur and corporation, we have to observe the entrepreneur in the small business he calls his own.

Joseph A. Schumpeter has pointed out that the entrepreneur is the man responsible for combining the other factors of production so as to produce a profit. It is rare for an entrepreneur to be an entrepreneur all the time, and it is rare for anyone in a management or executive position not to be an entrepreneur at some time. The entrepreneur gets things done. He is not necessarily the idea producer (the inventor). He does not spend his time finding out how to do things or what to do; he spends his time *doing* what has to be done. It has been said that everything is possible to the man who doesn't have to do it. Few men are doers; few can cope with the resistances and difficulties which action always meets. The entrepreneur not only must allocate his resources (his production factors), but must use them in action. Moreover, he has to combine these resources in a superior way to make an above-average profit—or perhaps to make any profit at all.

23

He should not be confused with the worker or the capitalist or the landowner. He is different from them in personality and motivation as well as in function. Neither is he primarily a risk taker in a gambling sense. He shares with others the multiple risks of the business world.

The entrepreneur is not a creature of general envy. According to one expert, David McClelland, "I find them [entrepreneurs] bores. They are not artistically sensitive . . . kind of driven—always trying to improve themselves and find a shorter route to the office or a faster way of reading their mail . . . it's an efficiency kind of thing. . . ."[1] Said W. Daniel Waddell, 28-year-old chairman of *Shopper's Voice,* "The only way you can succeed without money or connections is insane perseverance in the face of total rejection."[2]

David Goodrich studied ten young entrepreneurs, all successful and all under the age of 30. He discovered that they never waste a minute. They shun liquor, cigarettes, and drugs—soft or hard. They do not indulge in golf, tennis, bowling, theatregoing, TV-watching, fishing, adultery, or social organizations. They take holidays only occasionally. They work hard to win. One of these young men had two slogans on the wall of his office which may typify the entrepreneurial attitude: "Show me a good loser and I'll show you a loser" and "The harder I work the luckier I get."

WHAT THE STUDIES SHOW

The number of experts on entrepreneurship is small. Two academic centers of study relating to the entrepreneur have been at Michigan State University and Harvard University.

[1] Quoted by George T. Harris, "In Quest—A McClelland Sketch," *Psychology Today* (January 1971), p. 38.

[2] Philip A. Dougherty, "Involving the Shopper in the Message," *New York Times* (March 18, 1973), p. 15.

The Michigan studies concentrated on small business entrepreneurs and their characteristics. The studies at Harvard and at the Research Center in Entrepreneurial History, a neighbor of Harvard, concentrated on the founders of large enterprises. But little work has been done by academicians on the entrepreneurial role in the established large corporations of today.

The study of the entrepreneur has engaged the attention of psychologists, sociologists, social psychologists, political scientists, anthropologists, historians, and others. Because the life of the individual entrepreneur has to be interpreted in terms of his personality and environment, both psychology and sociology are critical to an understanding of what drives him on.

In a comprehensive sociopsychological study by Collins, Moore, and Unwalla some basic personality and environmental characteristics of entrepreneurs have been exposed by means of personal interviews and the Thematic Apperception Test (TAT), a projective testing technique about which more later. In this study, trained interviewers were selected on the basis of their knowledge of business as well as their experience and ability in depth interviewing. They interviewed 150 Michigan small business entrepreneurs, exploring their sociological and psychological backgrounds and administering the psychological Thematic Apperception Test. The information sought included family background; financial, sales, and employment figures of their enterprises; patterns of their business organization; and their future plans. All had volunteered to respond, and most cooperated fully.

Information from Depth Interviews   Saint Augustine once observed, "Give me the first seven years and the Devil can have the rest." Studies of the childhood and adolescent life of entrepreneurs have time and time again revealed a pattern quite different from any that social workers would consider normal or desirable. In the study of Collins, Moore, and Unwalla, depth interviews revealed a consistent pattern. Entrepreneurs are often orphaned or half-orphaned. One or both parents are dead, or one (generally the father) was away from home for long periods of time (jail, army, merchant marine), or the father was psychologically away from home, or when the father was home he was often drunk or "the laziest man I ever knew." The budding entrepreneur was on his own, without paternal restrictions, and free to establish his own position in life. Common themes running through the biographies of successful entrepreneurs are the escape from poverty, the escape from insecurity, death of parents, parents who went away, parents who were sent away. Time and time again in interviews with successful entrepreneurs the theme is one of symbolic or actual rejection of the father.

Many examples can be cited where a strong father inhibits entrepreneurship. In many cases, the son of an entrepreneur is unable to carry on in his father's manner; but his own son, the grandson of the strong father, revives the ability. Take the case of the Fords: strong business founder, Henry; overshadowed son, Edsel; strong grandson, Henry II. In one large chemical company the entrepreneurial character has been kept alive because a daughter married a strong entrepreneurial type who could succeed to the top job. This is not to say the strategy was a deliberate one, but the family line of succession was effectively carried on through marriage.

Information from Projective Tests   The Thematic Apperception Test (TAT) is a well-known psychological test widely used for a variety of purposes. It is called a projective test because it causes the subjects to project their personalities, motivations, and fears.

TAT consists of a collection of pictures which have a structure, but are fuzzy in definition. One might see a picture of a tall man and short man (or boy). Their relationship—for example, whether they are talking to one another—is indicated. The respondent is asked to make up a story about the picture. What are the men doing? What are they saying? What will happen as a consequence of these actions or words? Tests such as TAT show that the stories almost always reflect the respondent's own needs and feelings, whether in an autobiographical manner or through the use of psychological symbols. As interpreted by the experts, TAT stories show the needs of a respondent with reference to his personal relations with others, his work, his values, his goals, and his objectives. A trained analyst, who knows how others have reacted to the same pictures, can relate the personality of the new respondent to that of past respondents. These and similar tests are described in more detail in the books by Bernard Murstein and Johnson O'Connor.

The Thematic Apperception Test has shown these characteristics in entrepreneurs:

Lack of social mobility drives. Entrepreneurs put little stock in getting ahead. They do not strive for positions of authority and for the rewards associated with power and status.

Punishing pursuit of tasks and chronic fatigue. Entrepreneurs tend to push themselves to the point of fatigue, perhaps as a way to punish themselves. They do not "love" their work in the sense that they would be content to go on doing it indefinitely. Rather, when one job is done they look for other worlds to conquer.

Lack of problem resolution. Even in projective tests the entrepreneur notes problems but seldom resolves them. He sees the world as dichotomies—black or white, right or wrong.

Relations with subordinates. The entrepreneur tends to categorize subordinates at extremes of good or bad, depending upon whether they are viewed as possessing the good or bad aspects of self.

Relations with peers and partners. Generally enterpreneurs' relations with their partners are strained, but they have good relations with those outside the business.

Relations to authority. Entrepreneurs are generally unable to submit to authority in business and therefore try to set up their own businesses.

Remoteness of male authority figure. Entrepreneurs are seldom sought for help or looked upon as models to emulate. They generally regard male authority figures as a fraud, but an attractive one at that.

Views of females. Their views are motherly (good) or seductive (bad) with no in-between.

HOW PSYCHOLOGISTS VIEW THE ENTREPRENEUR

The psychologist's view of the entrepreneur will vary with the school of psychology (listed in order of historical development): psychoanalysis, behaviorism, and humanism. Each of the branches of psychology has made a contribution to our understanding of the entrepreneur because each considers man from a different perspective. Each school of psychology is appropriate to a certain time, a certain type of problem, and a certain point in human development. Humanism, for example, applies to man after he has satisfied his basic needs, and it deals with human potential rather than the human average.

Psychoanalytical School   The psychoanalytical school, founded by Sigmund Freud, takes the view that man's major motivations stem from deep inner drives and urges which are antisocial, irrational, and lacking in moral standards; these Freud said stem from the unconscious part of the psyche, which he called the id. These are checked by the superego, which acts to get individual conformity to the customs and morals imposed by parents and society. Between these two forces, Freud said, is the ego or conscious part of the psyche, which acts to resolve conflicts between id and superego. "Normal" people are those who have resolved these conflicts and do not have an excess of guilt or of frustrated and unsublimated desires.

The psychoanalyst's approach to the entrepreneur would be to classify him on a scale ranging from normal through neurotic to psychotic. It must be remembered that psychoanalysts deal almost exclusively with mentally distressed rather than so-called normal or average people, and this would affect their view of an entrepreneur. With this caveat in mind, let us consider the entrepreneurial personality in terms of Freudian psychology.

The entrepreneur has unresolved fears of his father, who was a weak figure in his life, and therefore cannot serve under a strong male figure or in an organization that is not his own but would represent a father image. Because of his father's weakness, say the Freudians, the entrepreneur must continually prove his masculinity. One way is to totally possess his business, because to share his power in his business would be a threat to his masculinity.

Both Freud and Alfred Adler had much to say about the power drive and its relation to the parent-child relationship. As Freud viewed human development, the infant has a great deal of power; he gets what he wants and has a number of adults at his beck and call. As he grows older, adults become less tolerant of his demands and now make demands of their own. The child has to surrender his power when this happens so as to preserve the affection and protection of his parents. If he is especially stubborn, or if his parents do not encourage him to make the switch, he will remain immature as he grows up.

The child tries to model himself after the parent of the

same sex. If the parent encourages this through attention, interest, and approval, the path to maturity is eased. If the model is unsatisfactory, instead of imitating the parent the child will lean over backward to become an opposite.

Alfred Adler, who was originally a follower of Freud but later established his own independent school of thought, placed great stress on the power drive. The infant has power over adults which he enjoys, said Adler, and often spends time as an adult trying to recapture this joy. The power drive is important in adults who consider themselves handicapped, whether or not they are handicapped in fact. The way they compensate for their inferiority complex is by trying to get power over people. The power motive is counterbalanced by a desire to cooperate with others, but it is strengthened in an adult who has had many disappointing contacts with untrustworthy adults.

Eric Berne, a Freudian psychiatrist who wrote the popular *Games People Play* and *What Do You Say After You Say Hello?* and was the founder of transactional analysis, suggested that people follow scripts written for them early in life by parents and other persons who are factors in their early environment. David McClelland has confirmed this by showing a relationship between the stories heard by children and their later motivations in life. Sid Rudin's focus was on people who became achievement-oriented or power-oriented. These qualities often determine how people act in business as well as in other facets in life. According to Rudin, achievers have a compulsion to be good at whatever they do. They follow scripts based on stories of success related by parents or educators, keep their feelings under careful control, and are likely to suffer from ulcers or high blood pressure. Power people respond to stories of risk and act in such a way as to attain power. They have a high death rate from such causes as suicide, homicide, and cirrhosis of the liver.

Behavioristic School   The behavioristic school, whose founder was John B. Watson and whose principal living exponent is B. F. Skinner, teaches that man's motivations are primarily the result of external environmental influences—in other words, that he develops by learning the appropriate responses to environmental stimuli. This school was heavily influenced by the experimental work of Ivan Pavlov on the conditioned reflex. Behaviorists do not consider deep motivations and look on normal behavior as average behavior.

Perhaps this school might favor a view of the entrepreneur that could be called the stranger hypothesis, based on the observation that minorities and foreigners give rise to a disproportionate share of entrepreneurial talent. In *Horatio Alger Is Alive and Well and Living in America,* David Goodrich points out that when he picked ten young entrepreneurial people at random as subjects for his book, half of them proved to be Jewish. Other observers have pointed out that Chinese became the entrepreneurs in Polynesia and East Indians became the entrepreneurs in Africa.

There are various explanations for the stranger hypothesis, all related to a response of people who come into a new environment from other cultural backgrounds. Because they are outsiders and minorities, they have limited opportunities in conventional channels, but entrepreneurial opportunities are more accessible. If legitimate entrepreneurial channels are closed, they may become entrepreneurial criminals.

A recent study by R. Lynn[3] attempts to link personality and national character with entrepreneurship. Even if such a link existed, McClelland has suggested it would vary over time with cultural cycle patterns. Moreover, those who emigrate to other countries may tend to be representative of the more entrepreneurial segments of the population and not of the population as a whole in their country of origin.

[3] *Personality and National Character.* Oxford: Pergamon Press (1971).

Humanistic School   The leader of the humanistic school
of psychology was Abraham Maslow. This school looks upon
man as a human being rather than as an animal, madman,
or machine. This school's viewpoint is less clearly defined than
the others, being a rather recent development of post-World
War II years. Maslow never wrote a comprehensive summary of his work, and such overviews are just starting to
appear.

Man's behavior is the result of internal drives and instincts
as well as external environmental determinants, say the humanists. He is motivated by hope, joy, and optimism. He is
self-motivated and self-governed. Psychology should not be
confined to the study of mentally disturbed people (as does
psychoanalysis) or of men as machines reacting to stimuli (as
does behaviorism). In fact, the real thrust of psychology
should be to show how man can reach his full potential, and
not merely adjust to being normal or average. As pointed out
in Chapter 1, where Maslow's hierarchy of needs is described,
man is moving to achieve a state of self-fulfillment, or self-
actualization, in which he can derive immense satisfaction
from realizing his capabilities.

In the humanistic view, the entrepreneur is a prime self-
actualizer who fulfills his destiny happily. He enjoys being
a doer, and his reward comes from meeting his goals.

B. F. Skinner's definition of behavior—activity which can
be seen and measured—is useful for management purposes
because it disregards the internal workings of attitudes, motivations, and personality. According to Skinner, when a desired
pattern of behavior is rewarded, it will tend to persist, and
will generate attitudes of success and adequacy.

However, Skinner's theory is inadequate because finding
what rewards will generate what behavior would be a long
and costly experience and because it ignores what Maslow's
hierarchy has shown—that the nature of these rewards

changes with time. Business will have problems unless its rewards are keyed to needs on the hierarchical scale.

THE ENTREPRENEUR'S RELATIONS
WITH SUPERIORS

At first glance, the preceding discussion of the entrepreneurial personality may seem academic. Obviously, we are not
dealing in hard facts, but in hypotheses and theories. However,
theories can be useful in selecting strategies when there are
no facts to go on. For example, when an entrepreneur who
has trouble submitting to a male authority figure is assigned
to work under an authoritarian boss, the result can be disaster.
A strategy to counter this difficulty could help hold acquired
entrepreneurs.

One highly successful organization that manages more than
120 entrepreneurs whose companies it acquired is U.S. Industries. Its method of operation is described in a later chapter,
but it is appropriate here to examine the psychological aspects
of this success. U.S. Industries has combined its acquired entrepreneurs into peer groups that meet once a year at a president's council and consider one another's business results in
detail. Prestigious titles abound. Each division has a president,
possibly a chairman, and several vice presidents, but there
are only 95 people in corporate headquarters.

The U.S. Industries company organization can be compared to a group of grown-up brothers who get along without
a father, rather than to a family of sons under an authoritarian
father. Brothers can be highly critical of each other without
arousing deep psychological fears. As a matter of choice, because of psychological and environmental factors, it is easier
for entrepreneurial managers to get along together in a
brother-brother relationship than in a father-son relationship.

FUTURE SOURCES OF ENTREPRENEURSHIP

Is the entrepreneur disappearing? The experts have suggested that the entrepreneur needs to react against a poor father figure. If that is so, will we find a continuing source of poor father figures? In the thirties we had the depression, which caused many fathers to appear as failures in the eyes of their children. However, if weak father images are needed, perhaps we shall have no lack in the seventies. For example, divorces are running almost 800,000 per year, with more than 60 percent involving children. The divorce rate is almost one-third of the marriage rate, and moving up. Also, in 1970 27 percent of all black families were headed by women.

On the other hand, the research may be misleading in linking the entrepreneur with a poor father image. It may be that an entrepreneur would either react against a very unsuccessful or emulate a very successful father figure. If we interview successful entrepreneurs of recent years, we are likely to uncover unsuccessful father figures because (1) many of the entrepreneurs grew up in the depression of the thirties when so many fathers had difficulty in supporting their families, (2) the sons of successful fathers would tend to go into their fathers' businesses or into professions for which their father could afford to prepare them.

The Effect of Business Education   Business education at the college level, and especially at the graduate level, appears to discourage entrepreneurship. Most business education is aimed at preparing students to work for others, and few evince any interest in being entrepreneurs.

Recently one of us interviewed about a hundred graduate business students, all of whom had spent some time working in business. All had thought about starting their own business, but none had. About half wanted to work for large companies, half for small companies; none wanted to start their own business.

The students felt that those who did start their own business were motivated by frustration in their work or by a desire to make more money than they could as employees. They themselves did not want to go into business because they saw four strong barriers to success: (1) The need for large initial capital; (2) a low ratio of reward to risk and a low chance of success; (3) a lack of business experience; and (4) a long period of years to achieve success.

When asked why they did not consider a franchise, such as the type of hamburger franchise which had made many people wealthy, the graduate business students had a negative reaction. In their view this kind of entrepreneurship, regardless of the monetary reward, was beneath their dignity.

Women as Entrepreneurs   Although a number of women have been successful entrepreneurs, the sample is too small for meaningful conclusions. As more women are drawn into the management and as their orientation relative to the business world changes, we can expect to hear of more women entrepreneurs. Women have been held back, not only by discrimination but by their environmental psychological set. According to the 1972 census, women make up almost 40 percent of the labor force, but only about 3 percent of working women are managers and administrators. Men in this classification outnumber women by more than five to one, a ratio only slightly changed in favor of women in the past 25 years.

Among top executives of large American companies, a *Fortune* survey shows men outnumbering women by about 600 to 1.[4] In the 1,220 largest U.S. corporations filing with the

[4] Wyndham Robertson, "The Ten Highest-Ranking Women in Big Business," *Fortune* (April 1973), pp. 80–89.

Securities and Exchange Commission and listing their three highest-paid officers, there were 6,500 men and 11 women on the list. These women are capable, hard-working executives. Three were co-founders of companies; one started her own company; five were members of families that owned the companies they worked in; and two moved up in an existing company hierarchy. Most combined careers and families. Eight are mothers. Only one was divorced, and she was happily remarried. Only one has never married. Only two are college graduates.

Among highly successful business women there is a recognition that for most women, interest and aspirations in business are low. In the *Fortune* survey Tillie Lewis, who founded the $100 million plus Tillie Lewis Foods, says: "Women may get to the top of the heap at some low level, but they don't try to move up to the next plateau. Somehow they're not *inspired*." Bernice Lavin, who runs Alberto-Culver jointly with her husband, finds many women unwilling to take on responsibility and fearful of mistakes: "A lot of girls want to be secretaries and that's it."

Matina Horner, psychologist and president of Radcliffe College, has identified the "motive to avoid success," to which women especially fall prey. Both men and women may be afraid of the costs of reaching the heights of ambition, achievement, and accomplishment. However, men are forced by the pressures of social and family responsibilities to face their fears and conquer them. Women are not so challenged. On the contrary, from childhood on, women are pressured away from business and toward the home. Only those who have to work—the poor and the disadvantaged—can altogether overcome their sense of guilt in pursuing and achieving business success. On the other hand, women have a need to be successful in their home life, whereas men do not; they get no extra credit for being good husbands or fathers.

In 1971, less than 3 percent of women college graduates earned their degrees in business, as compared to 22 percent for men. Business is the largest single major for men, education for women (36 percent of women graduates, less than 10 percent of men). However, increasing numbers of women are now headed for business schools. About 8 percent of those taking the exam to qualify for graduate business school in 1972 were women, two and one-half times the number five years previously. Until 1963, Harvard Business School accepted no women students. Ten years later 7 percent of the first-year students were women, almost double the 1972 number. Similarly, 13 percent of Columbia Graduate Business School's students entering in 1973 were women, two and one-half times the number five years previously. Dean Lawrence Fouraker of the Harvard Business School says there is a problem in getting women to enroll. "Women undergraduates aren't enthusiastic about business and it's hard to change that. But we are gradually getting more women. A lot of old myths are being destroyed."[5]

We know little about how women react to authority figures and how men would react to women as bosses. Dr. Muriel James, director of the Transactional Analysis Institute, Lafayette, California, said at the 1973 annual personnel conference of the American Management Associations: "A woman would rather work for a man than for a woman. In each case they want to get away from their mothers. Besides, men are easier for women to manipulate than other women are."

Basically, as a minority wanting to enter business life in a capacity of responsibility and authority, women should tend to increase the supply of entrepreneurs. It will take time to demonstrate whether this will actually be the case.

[5] Gerry Nadel, "For Harvard MBAs, the Bids Are High," *Women's Wear Daily* (April 27, 1973), p. 44.

CHAPTER 3

THE HIERARCH

In the preceding chapter the unique personality of the entrepreneur was unfolded. In this chapter he will be contrasted with the hierarch, the person who typically rises to the top in the large corporation. Can the entrepreneur be fitted into the large corporation to the benefit of both?

THE BIG BUSINESS SETTING

A place has to be found for the entrepreneur within the social structure of big business if he is to make a contribution to it. This makes it important to understand the setting and the psychology of those who occupy positions of power and have to be motivated to action by the entrepreneur. The term *business hierarchs* has been used by several authors to describe executives in large established businesses.

The structure in most big businesses is not organized around an entrepreneurial function. Rather, employees and executives alike become associated with such functional interests as production, marketing, and engineering. There appears to be someone responsible for everything except entrepreneurship. A further complication, according to William H. Whyte, author of *The Organization Man,* is the "fealty" which inculcates deference for elders and compels employees to stand in line for promotion. For an entrepreneur to get off the ground in an established organization he must overcome or learn to live with the characteristics of the establishment. These are:

Tradition. In big business, entrepreneurs face a tradition of longevity and conformity which few have managed to change.

Division of functions. Because of the functional division of work in most large companies, the entrepreneur finds it difficult to figure out who the decision makers are.

Social structure. The social structure in big business stresses getting along, going through channels, and not rocking the boat. Often leaders of functions strive to strengthen their own domains rather than the business as a whole.

Hierarchs and entrepreneurs reach top positions in business by different routes. The business hierarch climbs to the top through an established social structure, using the basic skills of occupational proficiency and social ability. Being less socially inclined, the entrepreneur generally builds his position by making deals—by pulling together combinations of men, money, and materials which contribute to profit.

Emotional and personality differences between entrepreneurs and business hierarchs point up some of the problems in fitting them together in a business. Some of the differences follow:

- Business hierarchs appear to strive ceaselessly to rise in their social positions, whereas entrepreneurs do not.
- Business hierarchs appear able to organize unstructured situations and to see the implications to their organizations. They can make decisions. Entrepreneurs, on the other hand, tend to be unsure of themselves and unable to make decisions, at least in test situations.
- Successful business executives appear willing to stay put in organizations, whereas entrepreneurs appear to be always on the move, restless to go on to new fields of endeavor.

- Business hierarchs appear to adapt readily to authority, whereas entrepreneurs rebel.

Conflicting Socioeconomic Backgrounds There are substantial differences in the socioeconomic status of entrepreneurs and large company executives. In *The Enterprising Man,* Collins et al. reported that of 150 entrepreneurs selected at random in Michigan, 20 percent were immigrants and 35 percent sons of immigrants, as compared to 5 and 20 percent for business executives and about 7 and 17 for the population as a whole. Similar results were found in other studies. Nor is birthplace the only difference between entrepreneurs and hierarchs. Studies show substantial differences in a variety of other characteristics, including religion, ethnic group, and socioeconomic class of parents.

The entrepreneur and the hierarch must inevitably clash because their perspectives on business and their role in it are poles apart. The hierarch in the large organization spends a great deal of time jockeying for position and playing politics. What is more, he is always asking himself of any action he contemplates: "How will it affect me and my position in the organization?" rather than: "How will this contribute to the goal?" To the entrepreneur, in contrast, politics, poor communication, and basic defects in company structure can be the cause of intolerable friction.

The Coper The business hierarch is only one variety of corporate executive who clashes with the entrepreneurial personality. Actually, many corporate executives become copers. A coper may be the corporation manager who holds his job because of the people he knows rather than what he can do, is content with inaction, and thinks mainly about job security. Or he may be a highly competent but frustrated manager whose latent talent has never been tapped. No one asks copers what they could or could not accomplish. They spend most of their time fighting a system that forever questions or challenges their competence and honesty. They are objects of suspicion instead of trust. They are managed from above with a heavy-handed top-down approach by corporate staffers who become their enemies instead of their allies. Their method of coping may proceed along these lines: "Tell us what you want to be told, and we'll tell you. Give us the forms, and we'll fill them out. If you want summaries, we'll give you summaries; if you want volumes, we'll give you volumes. We'll measure the unmeasurable; we'll drown you in data."

The coper may bring interest and variety to his work by playing practical jokes. Witness the auto assembly worker who fixes a car so that stepping on the accelerator blows the horn or sets the windshield washer and wipers in motion or who glues his fellow assemblers' toolboxes to the floor.

The corporate coper thrives where the entrepreneur dies.

LACK OF KNOWLEDGE OF ENTREPRENEURS

Unfortunately, today's business hierarchs have given little thought to the process of entrepreneurship and have had little exposure to the thoughts of others who have studied the field. Few of the articles and books concerned with entrepreneurship have been made readily accessible to businessmen. Some of the books are written by social scientists in a jargon that only other social scientists can understand, and articles appear in scholarly journals rarely seen by business executives. The only business magazine that has carried relevant articles—about 15 of them—in the past 25 years is the *Harvard Business Review*. Most businessmen are unaware of the studies carried out at the Research Center in Entrepreneurial History in Cambridge, Massachusetts, and at Michigan State University in Lansing.

For this reason, corporate executives are often confused as to what "entrepreneur" and "entrepreneurial" mean, how to identify and control entrepreneurship, and how it can be of value to the large corporation. Recently the executive vice president of a major U.S. corporation, a man who has spent 28 years as a hierarch, said about his company, "We must be entrepreneurs." His explanation for this assertion was that large companies must place a premium on flexibility and speed in decision making. This executive was talking only in terms of ends, not of means. He seems to be aware of the benefits of the entrepreneurial atmosphere, but probably knows little about the kind of persons he needs to create such an atmosphere and attain such results.

FITTING THE ENTREPRENEUR INTO THE HIERARCHY

Recently the 48-year-old president of a large corporation met with the 60-year-old owner and founder of a small business he was trying to acquire. The meeting degenerated into a shouting match, with the entrepreneur yelling: "We want to retain our independence. What happens to wild birds when they are caged?" To which the excitable hierarch responded: "They foul their nest, you old buzzard."

In this instance the two men did eventually come to terms. But the story nevertheless illustrates a point: that entrepreneurs and hierarchs do not easily understand or appreciate each other.

In an attempt to learn how entrepreneurs fared in large corporations, we queried 50 large chemical process companies selected from the *Fortune* 500 list, asking the following question:

Through direct hire or through acquisition of businesses, your company has undoubtedly employed men who have successfully demon-

strated superior entrepreneurial accomplishments in companies considerably smaller than yours. Can you comment on their adjustment to
the larger organization giving special attention to these points:
    a. Did they continue to demonstrate entrepreneurial attitudes
       in the large company environment?
    b. Were they able to transfer their entrepreneurial spirit to others
       in your company?

It was the intention of this question to determine whether
the respondents felt that entrepreneurship could be purchased
and whether entrepreneurs of proven ability could convey
their skills by education or inspiration to others in the large
company. The answers were quite controversial, some claim-
ing great success for the acquired entrepreneur in the larger
firm while others indicated only failure in adjustment.

About 20 percent of the respondents said they had little or
no experience in acquisitions and thus disqualified themselves
as experts. Another 20 percent appeared to have convincing
experience which proves that entrepreneurship cannot be purchased or transferred. In contrast, 60 percent believe entrepreneurship can be purchased and transferred, with many exceptions. The bothersome aspect of the negative replies is that
they came from several firms that have been conspicuously
successful in growth by acquisition. Two of the most pessi-
mistic replies came from highly successful acquirers. From a
firm that has grown considerably faster than its class in the
industry:

    a. Those people acquired through acquisition did not on the whole
       last very long in our Corporation. Those who did stay tended to
       be effective only within the framework of the acquired activity.
    b. I would have to say that they *were not successful* in transferring
       this spirit to others.

From another of Wall Street's favorites which has acquired
dozens of corporations over the past several years:

The answer is difficult and complex. Quite often when we have acquired a smaller company, the owner/manager, or "entrepreneur," has been unable to operate within the environment of the large organization. He is often not skilled at or attuned to the reporting needs and capital investment studies which large companies need in order to operate on the basis of solid management information. Entrepreneurs are often men who founded businesses of their own because of their inability, for one reason or another, to work successfully for others. When a smaller concern is acquired by a large company, this kind of entrepreneur usually has difficulty in adjusting to his new reporting relationships and to submitting to some control from a higher authority. Furthermore, he has often, in the sale of his company, become independently wealthy. Sometimes, too, his motivation in selling has been that he has reached an age approaching retirement, may have no strong successors, and may wish to convert his investment into the shares of a company whose stock is widely traded.

In sum, we have not had good experience in retaining the entrepreneurs of acquired businesses even though, in all instances, they have been given an unusual degree of operating autonomy. With few exceptions, these men have usually retired within a year or two after the acquisition.

Perhaps as a final thought I should tell you that the entrepreneurs in small businesses are quite often, upon acquisition, incapable of directing the growth of the acquired company into a large business. They are men not always skilled in the art of delegation or in the development of able managers and professional men. The lack of these skills has usually inhibited the growth of the company to anything much beyond the limits of "one-man management."

Having reviewed two of the least favorable replies, it is useful to review a sampling of replies that show promise for developing entrepreneurial attitudes through acquisition. From a firm that has outpaced its competitors through dozens of acquisitions comes this comment:

We have acquired a few businesses whose success was largely the result of the entrepreneurial talents of one or two men in top management. I do not believe we would have justification for saying that they were able to transfer their entrepreneurial spirit or talents to others in the existing company but, on the other hand, it seems quite clear that these men have continued to demonstrate their entrepreneurial attitude within the larger company's environment. Fortunately, the larger company already had some entrepreneurial talent at hand.

From another firm demonstrating rapid growth through acquisition comes this:

In my judgment our batting average may be a little better than the average for large companies because we have had an unusual amount of growth and diversification with many opportunities to challenge enterprising men with an entrepreneurial flare. For example, a number of jobs which are new in nature have been established as we grew and diversified. Frequently the entrepreneurial person has been picked for these new jobs. Generally they have been very successful. There are a number of instances where they have installed their same type of spirit in their associates, and at the same time handled the intricate interrelationships which frequently exist in large enterprises.

There is another side of the picture as well. One entrepreneur who started and ran a small educational publishing business sold out to a large publisher, but found the relationship impossible. After a parting of the ways, he launched another publishing business of his own. Of his short relationship with his merger partner he said: "We found ourselves going to endless committee meetings discussing education with a capital 'E' and getting none of the financial support we had anticipated." Moreover, the parent company had an "arbitrary practice of assigning unrelated losses to each distinct operating unit."

An executive recruiter states that 25 percent of his assignments specify "entrepreneurial characteristics," yet he finds only one real entrepreneur among 150 in large corporations. He warns that firms that fail to set up a profit center for a newly hired entrepreneur within six months to a year will lose the entrepreneur to another company or perhaps to his own business. Entrepreneurs want to make profits; nothing else will satisfy.

Employers look for higher entrepreneurial quotients when they seek more growth from acquisitions, new divisions, or new products—or when a business recession puts pressure on management to cut losses and maintain profits. As an example, consider the case of one major corporation out of the many that have gone through executive shakeups as a consequence of the recession starting in 1969. Top executives who came from eastern private-school backgrounds had characterized the management hierarchy from the time the company was founded. In the shakeup they were replaced by new men described as brisk, tough, self-made, hard-nosed, effective dollars-and-cents men. The traditional managers from exclusive prep schools and prestigious colleges were competent and presentable, good men for good times. One such executive was described as "wonderfully decorative—a blond version of Errol Flynn—with a face that just cries out, '$70,000 a year.'" In contrast, the new men were tough men for tough times; their official corporate biographies ignored the fact that they had gone to public high schools. Thus when the chips are down the entrepreneur comes to the forefront because that is when performance, only performance, counts.

CHAPTER 4

FINDING AND TRAINING CORPORATE ENTREPRENEURS

THE QUALITIES that make the entrepreneur probably occur in less than 5 percent of the population. To a very large extent entrepreneurial qualities are brought out only when the cultural and family environment is suitable. In addition, the entrepreneur emerges only in the proper business environment. An inhibiting environment such as is often found in the very large company will stifle entrepreneurship.

SCREENING AND TESTING FOR ENTREPRENEURSHIP

For the most part, psychological and other screening tests have been inconclusive in identifying entrepreneurs. On the other hand, when successful entrepreneurs are tested on certain qualities as a group, their scores are different from those of other persons in business. This anomaly arises from the nature of entrepreneurial characteristics.

Because entrepreneurship seems to depend on a combination of personal characteristics, testing for it is as difficult as is testing for the rare talents of managers or salesmen. To illustrate the problem, a hypothetical situation can be postulated. Assume that a test for entrepreneurship is given to ten people and that half score 100 and the other half score 120. Of the ten, one becomes a successful entrepreneur. He scored 120. The test is repeated again and again, with the same results. For each ten tested, five score 100; of these five, none has entrepreneurial talents. The remaining five score 120, and one of them is an entrepreneur.

The test has shown a difference between entrepreneurs and others; but if it were to be used to find entrepreneurs, it would have a low reliability. Of those who score 120 (which includes all entrepreneurs), only one out of five will prove to be an entrepreneur. The other four who score 120 are not entrepreneurs.

On the other hand, none of those who score 100 are entrepreneurs. Thus the test can screen *out* those who cannot succeed as entrepreneurs. The chance that an entrepreneur is among those who remain is still small, though it is twice as great as it was before the test.

A projective test such as TAT, described in Chapter 2, might be useful in screening out those who are unlikely to become entrepreneurs or who actually want to avoid success. In a projective test the respondent may be asked to complete a story line, telling what happens next. Often respondents reveal their inclination to avoid success by the way they complete their story lines. For example, the story might start: "Jack is thinking of setting up his own business. . . ." The respondent who completes the story ". . . but he realizes he can make more money working for a large company" will not be an entrepreneur. Nor will the respondent who answers, ". . . because Jack will make a lot of money in his own business. . . ." As will be pointed out, money is not a prime entrepreneurial motivator. Potential entrepreneurs who complete their stories will reveal their entrepreneurial motivations, as described later in this chapter.

According to all the evidence, there is no single trait or set of traits which is always present in entrepreneurs and always absent in others. Moreover, there is no ideal executive for every organization and every situation. Successful executive performance depends on a complex series of actions taking place in a specific situation and within a fixed organizational structure. The entrepreneur cannot function in the wrong setting; his actions and behavior can be effective only when they are consistent with the situation. The best actor cannot improve a poor play, nor can the best entrepreneur perform in a hostile environment. He will be as out of place as the proverbial bull in the china shop.

QUALITIES OF THE CORPORATE ENTREPRENEURIAL MANAGER

The characteristics of successful and effective entrepreneurial managers in the large corporation include these five:

1. A need to manage and to have power over people
2. A need to achieve and to have fast, precise feedback of results
3. The capacity for empathy and an ability to deal with the emotions of others
4. The ability to carry out his job according to the needs of each task
5. A willingness to conform to corporate policies

Entrepreneurship is not restricted to business. Admiral Hyman Rickover, an outspoken and unpopular entrepreneur in the U.S. Navy, was grudgingly promoted to admiral late in his career. The nuclear-powered submarines in today's

Navy testify to his success. His rules for success were simple: (1) The interests of the project come before the interests of any members of the project; (2) trouble must be dealt with, not buried; (3) the leader must be involved in the work. Such rules would probably have made him a successful business entrepreneur as well. Considering that he had to buck the Navy promotion system, the seniority system, waiting-in-line, and religious prejudice, Rickover has been an unusual entrepreneur, to say the least.

Because of the difficulty in finding the right combination of the qualities that constitute entrepreneurship, a job that requires this talent may end up in the hands of more than one person. Alberto-Culver, an entrepreneurial cosmetics company, is run by a husband-and-wife team. Leonard Lavin, president, is the idea man of Alberto-Culver; and Bernice Lavin, treasurer and secretary, handles the administrative side. They have worked together for 25 years, not only building a company but raising three children as well. They even eat lunch together every day. There are several such husband-and-wife teams in business.

For this kind of synergy the entrepreneurial partners have to be more than friends or relatives; they have to have complementary skills. Edwin H. Land, who invented the Polaroid-Land camera, found others who could furnish the financial skills he lacked. Chester Carlson, the inventor of xerography, found an entire team ready to move his invention at the Haloid Company in Rochester—now Xerox—and a very entrepreneurial team it turned out to be.

A Need to Manage   Entrepreneurial managers have a need to manage; that is, a need to have power over people. They work hard to reach positions where they exercise authority over a large staff. One byproduct is that they are not prepared either to be authoritatively managed from above by their superiors or to delegate to their subordinates. They hold tight reins on their authority and shy away from consultative or permissive management techniques in dealing with subordinates, especially when their authority is challenged.

A Need to Achieve   Entrepreneurs have a strong desire for achievement, for doing a good job. Profit is one measure of how well the job is done, but it is not the only one. Under capitalism the measure is profit; under communism it may be a quota. Both systems need the entrepreneur. But profit or a quota is the measure, not the goal. People with high achievement drives think in terms of doing or achieving, not merely of measuring.

Entrepreneurial managers have a view of achievement different from that of professionals. The professional scientist wants to achieve, but in terms of scientific breakthroughs, reputation—intangibles that cannot be measured in the quantitative way that a profit measures the achievement of the entrepreneur.

The entrepreneur typically has a picture or concept of his mission in his mind. He looks for certain criteria in his job that can best satisfy his needs and drives.

1. The entrepreneur wants individual and personal responsibility for managing and running a business situation. He is not a gambler because the outcome of a gamble is a matter of chance, not of ability. Nor is he a buck-passer. If he thinks a thing can be done, he sets out to do it.

2. The entrepreneur sets moderate achievement goals and can evaluate his risks. He wants neither the easy routine job nor the too-hard-to-solve problems. He operates in the area where he knows he can be effective without being underutilized.

3. The entrepreneur is results-oriented rather than efforts-oriented. He measures his accomplishments by the profits he

makes, not by the hours he puts in. He may talk about his efforts because he has to feel he is working up to his physical capacity or even overextending himself. He complains of over-work, but he knows that only one measure is relevant to his efforts: the profit he makes.

4. The entrepreneur cannot get along without profits as a *concrete* feedback as to how well he is doing. He wants a lot of feedback, and he wants it quickly. The typical busi-nessman in a setting of sales and profit graphs fulfills the vision of the entrepreneur. But profits are not the motivator. The motivator is the will to achieve. Profit and monetary or status rewards are merely the measure of success.

The need to achieve has been listed following the need to manage, to have power over people. The small company entre-preneur may reach a critical stage while the company is still small if he hasn't enough power drive, despite a strong achievement drive. When the enterprise gets beyond the point of being a one-man operation, the entrepreneur may lack the drive to assemble the kind of management team that is vital to continued growth. It's not that he doesn't wish to delegate; it's that he doesn't feel a need to control and manage people.

David McClelland suspects that corporate managers are more power-motivated than achievement-motivated and that the reverse is true for entrepreneurs. In the United States the trend is for achievement motivation to decline and power mo-tivation to increase. In *The Achieving Society,* McClelland points out that in 1925 the United States was high in achieve-ment but low in power motivation. By 1950, power motivation had gone up sharply but achievement motivation had stayed about the same or slipped.

Student radicals are likely to be the children of educated professionals, who tend to be permissive parents and encour-age self-reliance and achievement. Limited studies of student radicals by David Winter and his colleagues at Wesleyan University indicate student radicals tend to be high in achievement motivation and lower in power motivation—the reverse of students who are anti-radical. The radicals show their entrepreneurship in the way they build new organizations and institutions. They would sometimes rather go out on the street and sell articles they have made themselves than work for a large corporation. Their achievement motive is high; their power motive is low.

In small companies, the higher the achievement motivation, the higher the person tends to be in pay and position. The company president, who is often the founder as well, appears to be highest in achievement score. In large companies, only through the middle brackets does achievement score relate to position and pay. But the very top managers are only average in achievement score, either because they are successful enough to relax or because they are higher than others in power drive. Power is the key. As Bertrand Russell has said: "Power is the ability to move people."

Monetary and status rewards, as mentioned, are not motivators, but merely confirm the success that the achiever sees mirrored in the profits he earns for himself or his company. Unfortunately a high salary does not make a manager and can in fact destroy perspective. The person who accidentally arrives at a high salary level thinks he is good because his earnings tell him he is. And the same is true for the entrepreneur who becomes an instant millionaire through acquisition. Money has been his measure of success, and instant money makes him instantly successful. All his inadequacies seem to disappear, and he refuses to believe that luck may have played a major part in his success. His new-found fortune tells him that he's good and that his wealth is attributable to his own brains and energy. He may continue to move ahead fast for a time, but if things go wrong, he will come down to earth with a thud.

A Capacity for Empathy   To succeed, the corporate entrepreneur must be able to cope with the emotions of others. He has to get his subordinates to respond to his wishes and his superiors to grant his desires. He is in the position of General Eisenhower when he moved into the presidency. When he was elected, Harry S Truman said: "Poor Ike. When he was a general, he gave an order and it was carried out. Now he is going to sit in that big office and he'll give an order and not a damn thing is going to happen."

The nature of empathy is easily misunderstood. One young management trainee said: "I don't want to be a manager, I want to be liked." Being liked is not the only way to get people to do things; it may even be the wrong way. Empathy is the ability to put oneself in another person's shoes, to share his feelings or ideas. Empathy means an understanding of what motivates subordinates. Whether a manager is liked, admired, or respected doesn't matter so long as he gets results from his subordinates. Otherwise he gets only sabotage, whether deliberate or not. Similarly, he must relate to his superiors, put himself in the shoes of the people who give the orders, so as to understand and appreciate their viewpoint.

The Ability to Perform   The successful entrepreneurial manager must not only have drives toward achievement and power, he must also have the ability to perform. Ability does not necessarily have to be of a specialist or technical nature, unless this directly pertains to the task at hand. Persons with high power drives may assume an early lead in promotion into management, but they may also disappear rapidly from the management ranks because of their failure to perform. Wishing doesn't make it so. Desires and ambitions will not suffice, no matter how much they drive the individual, unless they are backed by ability. Fidel Castro had the drive to achieve control of Cuba, but he has lacked the ability to make Cuba an economic success.

A Willingness to Conform   The ideal corporate entrepreneur must be as satisfied to conform to policy as he is to make policy. In other words, he must adapt his personal behavior to the requirements of corporate policy. He may be more amenable to this if he participates in the formulation of policy and understands the need as well as the justification for it. If he cannot adapt, it doesn't matter how much money he makes or what rewards he receives; he will become restive within the restraints of the corporate atmosphere. The high power self-starter, the highly aggressive manager cannot satisfy corporate requirements if he cannot respond to instructions. Even more important, he cannot function within the corporate organization if he cannot take orders.

The primary problem of the entrepreneur in the large corporation is relations with his superiors. This may be because he has had from childhood an unusual degree of independence. He is used to fending for himself, making his own decisions, setting his own standards and his own goals, demanding a level of achievement that can be attained only when one's inner drives are strong.

None of this would have been possible had the entrepreneur had a dominant or authoritarian father. And none of it would be possible under a domineering and authoritarian boss. That an entrepreneur must conform to fundamental corporate policy is unquestioned. But he cannot put his entrepreneurial skills to work in an atmosphere of excessive conformity or constraint.

GRADUATE BUSINESS EDUCATION

There is no direct relationship between performance in school or in training programs and success in management, according to Professor J. Sterling Livingston of the Harvard Business School. Courses of study for the degree of master of business administration do not teach students how to manage. Formal programs emphasize the development of problem-solving and decision-making skills, not the development of managerial skills. What are these undeveloped managerial skills? (1) skill in identifying the problems that need to be solved; (2) skill in planning for the attainment of desired results; (3) skill in carrying out operating plans once they are made.

Success in management depends on finding and exploiting opportunities and on identifying and dealing with problems *before* they become critical. Peter Drucker had something to say about this in *Managing for Results:*

> All one can hope to get by solving a problem is to restore normality . . . results must come from the exploitation of opportunities. "Maximization of opportunities" is a meaningful, indeed a precise, definition of the entrepreneurial job. . . . The pertinent question is not how to do things right, but how to find the right things to do. . . .[1]

Strangely enough, neither chief executives in business nor graduate business students consider the ability to manage a high-ranking goal of graduate business education. In a recent survey by Professor Thomas L. Wheelen of the University of Virginia's McIntire School of Commerce, both chief executives and graduate business students agreed on two top goals in M.B.A. studies: (1) training to develop analytical and problem-solving abilities; (2) training to develop an understanding of the political, social, and economic environment of business.[2]

The area of greatest disagreement was the goal of training for responsible management positions. Chief executives ranked this tenth of eleven goals, whereas students ranked it fifth.

---

[1] New York: Harper & Row (1964), p. 5.
[2] "MBA Degree Programs . . . Is There a Generation Gap?" *Atlanta Economic Review* (November-December 1972), pp. 16, 17.

Harry A. dropped out of college after two years and started his own company, which reached $25 million in annual sales in less than ten years. Suddenly he became big business. He hired Phil C., a young Harvard M.B.A. one year out of school, who had just left his first job with a big company. Harry worked on instinct, but Phil liked charts and systems; he didn't particularly like people. He drew charts and talked a lot about cash flow and decision trees. He told Harry that he must delegate more. Harry hired several vice presidents but didn't enjoy delegating, and within a month he was arguing vehemently with his new staff. Phil, who knew little about people and motivation, recommended switching the sales force from commission to salaries. When Harry took Phil's advice, two salesmen quit and formed their own businesses, in competition with Harry. Luckily for Harry, he also argued with Phil, the young Harvard M.B.A. Phil was fired and went back to work for a big company, and Harry went back to relying on his instinct and his entrepreneurial talents.

Preoccupation with problem solving and decision making develops analytical ability but leaves underdeveloped the ability to take action and get things done. The behavior required to solve problems that already have been uncovered and to make decisions on the basis of facts gathered by others is quite different from the behavior required for other management functions.

In the classroom, students explain and defend their reasoning, but they do not have to carry out their decisions or plan implementation or deal with human emotions. On the other hand, managers need to be able not only to analyze data in financial statements and written reports, but also to scan the business environment for less precise clues that a problem exists. They must be able to read meaning into environmental and competitive changes that may not show up in operating statements for months or years. They manage by perception.

This ability to see patterns in events probably comes only through experience. Management cannot be learned second-hand. It entails the use of intuitive judgment or hunches, which really means the ability to see patterns rather than individual events—the forest rather than the trees. Hunches are arrived at through personal observation of the business environment, its characteristics and its reactions. The observer notes the influence of changing conditions, but he may not set out to discover or use exact quantitative relationships to interpret them, even though he may be cognizant of these relationships and be able to derive valuable clues from them. The psychologist calls this a gestalt, a total view which is deeper and greater than the sum of the individual parts.

A similar phenomenon exists among the very top chess grand masters, who can easily beat a computer at the game. One said that when he looked at the board in play, he saw power patterns which appeared to glow around the pieces, the brightness of the glow being an indication of the strength of the positions. This chess master could envisage how possible moves would affect his power pattern as compared to that of his opponent. But when the pieces were put on the board in a purely random way, the expert saw no glow and could not make any sense of the chessboard.

The experienced manager can make his hunches work in the same way that a driver can make a car go without knowing exactly how the engine was put together. But he will have no hunches without experience, intuition, know-how, and time for observation and reflection. Usually he cannot even explain his methods to others in terms of methodology or principles because his learning was by trial and error.

High grades in school and outstanding performance as accountant, engineer, or salesman reveal how able and willing a person is to perform assigned tasks. But these successes are not proof that a person can direct others to do the job. Certainly, education beyond an M.B.A. degree will not help. When asked about the value of a Ph.D. degree, one educator addressing an American Management Associations luncheon told about the Argentinian racehorse Cannonero II, which was given a Ph.D. by a Buenos Aires university after it had won both the Kentucky Derby and the Preakness. "It was the first time," the educator observed, "that the whole horse was awarded a Ph.D."

Executives are not the only ones unhappy about the M.B.A. Graduates show their dissatisfaction by frequent job-hopping when the economy is doing well. On the other hand, many business hierarchs prefer to hire the graduates of a leading business school. They're conservative in approach as well as in dress, good committee men, and good team men. As one Harvard M.B.A. put it: "The way I've got it figured, we're not the dashing tycoons, the individualists of the old days. Those individualists—when they were good, they were great, but when they were bad, they were horrid! We're good team men—and easier to live with."

Can these circumstances be changed? Perhaps, but it may be difficult. Apparently both hierarchs and business school students perceive current M.B.A. programs as desirable ones. Yet both are unhappy with some of the results. Perhaps the solution is to base management training on a different type of educational philosophy and curriculum. In military academies, cadets are trained in making decisions and leading groups. Can business school curricula be similarly structured? Which graduate business school will be the first West Point of capitalism?

MAKING THE RIGHT CHOICE

It is far easier to select entrepreneurial management personnel who have little chance of success than it is to make the right choice. In large corporations the choice may be made by staff, management development, or personnel department executives who have little contact with, or understanding of, entrepreneurial operations. Following are some of the people to consider, and some to avoid, in filling posts that require the qualities of an entrepreneur.

The Minority Group Member   Entrepreneurship appears to be more prevalent among minority and deprived groups than among other segments of the population. Entrepreneurial qualities may be high among persecuted minorities because they have been faced with so many challenges and among immigrants because they have had to surmount substantial barriers. Until recently, many large corporations discriminated against such minority groups. But their demonstrated superiority in this area is reason enough to give them careful consideration when entrepreneurship is at issue.

The Gambler   Many of us confuse the gambler personality with the entrepreneur. Entrepreneurs do not gamble; they take calculated risks. The gambler depends on sheer chance, without any control over the results, whereas the businessman has to evaluate the control risk. The confusion may arise because businessmen use the word "gamble" as a synonym for risk taking, as Bernard Baruch did to his regret on one occasion. As he tells the story, in 1909 J. P. Morgan's firm asked him to investigate a sulfur deposit, Bryan Mound. Baruch investigated, then told J. P. Morgan that the whole property could be purchased for $500,000. "I added that I was willing to 'gamble' half of this sum from my own funds. 'Gamble' was a poor choice of language. I should have said 'invest.' " "I never gamble," replied Mr. Morgan with a gesture that signified the interview was over, and the venture closed as far as he was concerned.

One characteristic of the entrepreneurial manager is that

he will not be happy with easily attainable or routine goals. He is very likely to give up the small bird in the hand for the elusive two in the bush. But this is not gambling; it is fitting his capabilities to a goal of proper size. In fact, the successful entrepreneur may be very naïve when it comes to gambling with his own money, as in the stock market, and is not likely to fare well unless he leaves it to the professionals. The skills needed to make money in the stock market are quite different from those of the entrepreneur.

Richard L. was a good salesman—so good that he rapidly rose to divisional president. At the first company Christmas party after he assumed control, Richard started a dice game in an adjoining room and spent the night gambling with some of his subordinates. Thereafter, sales meetings were followed by nightlong poker games. As head of his division, Richard introduced many startling innovations and earned a reputation for nerve and flair. But not all his innovations took hold and some were costly. Gradually the executives reporting to him were replaced by poker-playing friends. Richard did most of the work himself; his staff's function was to help him relax. Profits drifted downward. Richard talked well and managed to win the board's approval of even more startling innovations. He promised a big killing, but somehow it never materialized. Although the division didn't fall below the profit line, the return on capital was unacceptably low, and after two years Richard was politely fired. He talked his way into an even better-paying job as president of a medium-size company with $200 million in annual sales. Soon the firm was involved in a Canadian mining venture with high promise. But the deposit didn't pan out, losses showed up on the books, and Richard L. "resigned" after a two-year term.

The true gambler believes that he can foretell the outcome of a chance occurrence with absolute certainty. To him, gambling is a matter of faith. He does without wine, women, and song to satisfy his pathological compulsion to gamble. He is not the man who regularly places small bets on the horses or numbers and derives satisfaction from winning. The true gambler values the prize only before he has won, not afterward. He is not rational in evaluating his chance of success. He tends to play for high stakes and assume large risks, and as his losses mount, so do his hopes.

So ingrained in American tradition is the Puritan ethic that playing or gaming as a way to wealth and success is contrary to our cultural heritage. This prejudice extends to Wall Street and other financial centers, as is evident when Wall Street is portrayed in American literature. Novelists commonly speak of an individual's involvement with the stock market and financial circles as a form of personal corruption, wastefulness, and degeneracy. Typical plots show the naïve hero being seduced by the devil—in the form of a clever broker—into buying stocks and ending in ruin. The plot follows the Biblical story of Adam's temptation and fall or the tale of Faust's compact with the devil.

Recently the shoe industry was shocked to hear of the suicide of a man who had founded and run a company with almost $40 million in sales in 1973. He had borrowed money on his furniture in 1947 to start the company. His business life had been exemplary, and his company showed persistent steady growth. But he gambled in the stock market, and his gamble did not pay off. At age 50 he lost more than $7 million of the firm's funds in commodity trading and killed himself.

In contrast to the cautious man and the gambler, McClelland has found that if an entrepreneurial high achiever is put into an entirely novel situation, where he cannot gauge his chance of success because he has no previous applicable experience, he will plunge ahead and make more of the opportunity than the cautious man who insists on more facts or more time. Yet he shows prudence when the chances of success can be weighed. He will scorn the low return and the high-risk venture. He would seem best adapted to either (1) competitive ventures with a good return-to-risk ratio or (2) exploratory ventures where the chances of success and the returns are not yet determinable.

The Egomaniac   Sometimes an entrepreneur will ride roughshod over all opposition and tolerate little in the way of advice or criticism or orders from his subordinates or superiors because he believes he is surrounded by morons and idiots. Often this attitude is evidence of the failings of the egomaniac. Such a man transfers his own weaknesses and fears to superiors and subordinates, seeing his own weaknesses reflected in them. When he runs them down he is looking into a mirror and seeing there the roots of his own egomania: a deep fear that he will fail if he trusts or relies on others.

Dr. Walter C. Langer, a noted psychoanalyst who wrote *The Mind of Adolf Hitler* in 1943 as a secret wartime report for the Office of Strategic Services, quotes Adolf Hitler's words, which epitomize the entrepreneurial egomaniac: "I do not look for people having clever ideas of their own but rather people who are clever in finding ways and means of carrying out my ideas." To the egomaniac the only person with sense is himself.

The Security Seeker   The typical security seeker will ask about the pension plan rather than about opportunities. He will be frightened by offers of authority and responsibility, or he may try to buy security by making exorbitant demands or complicated long-term employment contracts. Such a person's entrepreneurial qualities have long been buried, if he ever had any, and he should be considered for a job only if it offers good fringe benefits, an entrenched seniority system,.

and no challenge. Not only is he no entrepreneur but he should not even be put to work in the vicinity of an entrepreneur.

The Crank   It is sometimes hard to separate the dedicated entrepreneur from the dedicated crank. A banker tells of a young man who was seeking money to make a material for facing bricks for buildings. "Do you have samples?" the banker asked. "I did," answered the investor, "but my mother was cleaning and threw them out." Similarly, in a big company, the persistent and dedicated promoter of a new idea may be completely wrong or a self-deceived crank. It would be disastrous to put a crank to work at an entrepreneurial task; that much is obvious. What is not so obvious and cannot be measured is the loss that could be sustained if an entrepreneur should be written off as a crank.

The Professional   Professionals do not have the same goals as entrepreneurs. They are committed to their profession—chemistry, engineering, accounting—whereas the entrepreneur, who has to spread himself thin, is forced to perform as many functions as his ability and energy will allow. The professional is devoted to doing things right; he doesn't care what it costs in time or money. The entrepreneur does care; he aims at doing the right things in the right sequence. Peter Drucker has said that finding the right things to do is a prime management function. The professional separates himself from decisions; the entrepreneur makes decisions. The professional is committed to his own technology or skills; the entrepreneur is committed to the needs of the market. The professional measures himself by his efforts; the entrepreneur measures himself by the results he achieves in terms of profit.

A research chemist's measure of his own performance is the number of patents he receives or the papers he publishes. A salesman's measure of his own performance is the number of pounds he sold or the number of calls he made. Not so the entrepreneur. His measure of performance is significant not only to him but to the corporation: profit.

Harold G., research director of a large electronics company, pointed with pride to his publications and patents. He was developing a large new area of inventions which were recognized as a major technological breakthrough. Harold held back on trying to commercialize his efforts because he wanted to make sure that he did enough research to establish an unassailable patent position, and he bitterly criticized commercial development people who wanted to reveal his developments to customers. When a market survey showed that customers were not interested in some of his developments, Harold said that the commercial people could still sell the product if they were capable of making the customers recognize their needs. Harold invented a new and unique analytical instrument. When it proved too complicated for use by technicians in the field, he blamed the customers for their lack of foresight and blamed the commercial development people for their lack of skill. When he resigned, he sent a letter to top management stating that the company did not have people capable of converting technical successes to commercial successes.

Some companies *have* made entrepreneurs out of professionals on a small scale. Moog, Inc.'s Controls Division in East Aurora, New York, has transformed four full-time and two part-time salaried computer programmers into freelance entrepreneurs who can bid on every new job. The result is improved conformance to time schedules, lower costs, and higher pay.

IS YOUTH A FACTOR?

Bradley Dewey Sr. was one of the founders of the Dewey & Almy Chemical Company in Cambridge, Massachusetts.

When he retired in 1952 at age 65 he was president, and Dewey & Almy was a good-size public company. In 1954 it was merged into W. R. Grace & Co. In the decade following retirement Dewey launched Bradley Container Company, now the Bracon Division of American Can Company, to make plastic tubes. When he sold his interest in Bradley Container he started a third company, Hampshire Chemical, to make specialty chemicals called chelates. Eventually, he sold Hampshire to W. R. Grace & Co., the second time Grace acquired a company in which he was a principal.

As Bradley Dewey demonstrated, age alone does not deteriorate those rare qualities which motivate the entrepreneur. Yet many people who have had the chance to be entrepreneurs and have failed because they lacked entrepreneurial qualities or abilities have had their failure blamed on aging.

Floyd Odlum set up a new $100 million land development business venture in 1973 when he was 81 years old. Fifty years earlier he had founded the notably successful Atlas Corporation when he was 31.

Toyoji Naito retired at 65 in 1946 as director of research of Kanebo, the second largest pharmaceuticals company in Japan. He acted as a consultant until 1952, when he founded the Eisai Company, a pharmaceuticals concern, with a capital of $2,500. In 1972 that company had sales of $100 million and was the fifth largest pharmaceuticals company in Japan.

The history of entrepreneurs reveals that they make their entrepreneurial qualities apparent at various ages. Some of them have spent as much as 20 years in seemingly aimless drifting and dragon-tilting before they struck a successful deal. For example, in the late thirties, Ray Kroc was Lily Tulip's Midwest sales manager selling paper cups. He "wanted adventure," so he struck out on his own, acquiring the rights to a machine that would mix six malted milks at a time. He was modestly successful until 1954, when, at the age of 51, he sold eight of his malted milk machines to a drive-in restaurant in San Bernadino, California, owned by two brothers named McDonald. The brothers had franchised six stores. Ray Kroc acquired the right to sell McDonald franchises, and in 1973 his McDonald stock was worth more than $500 million.

T. H. White has said: "There is a thing called knowledge of the world which people do not have until they are middle aged. It is something which cannot be taught to younger people because it is not logical and does not obey laws which are constant. It has no rules."[3]

When Governor Ronald Reagan of California celebrated his 62nd birthday, he said he would not be too old to run for president in 1976 at the age of 65. He disagreed with those "who believe that just when you've learned the rules you're too old to play the game. . . . I don't think you kiss anybody off because they're too young or too old. . . ."[4]

TRAINING NEW ENTREPRENEURS

Corporate entrepreneurs have to be trained and tested on the job, just as the small business entrepreneur is tested in the real business world. In the corporation environment, the entrepreneur has to be assigned management tasks and responsibilities in such a way as to simulate the small business environment. Today's business school cannot provide the training because it is too far removed from the practical problems of business and may not even know what it is that the entrepreneurial business executive will have to know.

One publisher has said that only about 20 percent of executives buy business books. Most of these executives are not young, having been in executive jobs for at least ten years.

Perhaps you have to be a little older before you know what it is you don't know.

One approach to training for entrepreneurial management has been suggested by David McClelland and David Winter. In *Motivating Economic Achievement* they describe a course they ran in India under a Carnegie Foundation grant to train entrepreneurs. The Indian trainees were given the Thematic Apperception Test, which asked them to write a story about a picture. High achievers tended to relate the story to work and business; low achievers related it to other interests— perhaps family or leisure activities.

The trainees were shown the relation between achievement drive and the images they had developed in the test and then were asked to rewrite their stories to deliberately attain higher achievement scores. In other words, they were asked to consciously direct their fantasies toward business. Next they participated in a business game that put a premium on entrepreneurial qualities: setting their own goals, keeping the goals moderate, taking personal responsibility for solving problems at moderate risk, and getting quick feedback.

Although the experimental course lasted only ten days, within the next two years those Indian businessmen who took the course started four times the number of businesses, invested twice as much money, and created twice as many new jobs as those who did not take the course.

Michael Argyle suggests that McClelland's success in India may be due to the learning of new management techniques rather than to any increase in motivation. However, McClelland reports that he taught no new management techniques, except possible brainstorming, which took less than one of the ten training days. And no one has demonstrated that brainstorming is a good technique in training entrepreneurs, although it has other values.

Today, new approaches to business education are required if entrepreneurial management is the object. The work of

McClelland and Winter in India offers one approach. As suggested earlier, perhaps some of the techniques of West Point in teaching leadership and decision making might be introduced. There is a great deal of thinking about these problems to be done. It may be, as the existentialist philosophers say: "Whatever you do, you become."

In a more recent training program, Douglas Durand worked with prospective black entrepreneurs. The training program consisted of two parts: achievement motivation training and management development training. The motivation segment was based on the methods proposed by McClelland. The management development segment covered accounting, finance, management, and marketing. Participants increased both their achievement motivation scores and their involvement in business activities. The data support the conclusion that behavior change can result from training programs which pay attention to psychological considerations and provide management knowledge as well. Groups which received only one or the other kind of training engaged in less business activity than groups which received both kinds of training.

The "need for achievement" concepts of Professor McClelland are also being used in a training program at TRW's Systems Group at Redondo Beach, California, by William Curra, organization development manager for System Development Corporation, and Dr. R. Douglas Brynildsen, organization development manager at the TRW Systems Group. Career achievement workshops have been set up to identify occupational profiles in people and help change these profiles where change could be beneficial. The steps in the motivation training process are threefold:

1. Giving the employee a greater understanding of basic career motivations and their own perception of these motivations
2. Providing a high-achieving model

3. Helping employees to change if they want to, and in the direction they want to change, to match their own profile to the high-achiever profile

The program includes a preliminary Thematic Apperception Test in which participants' profiles are measured, an orientation meeting for further testing and discussion, and a two and one-half day workshop. While results have not been measured quantitatively, the performance of employees appears to improve substantially after they attend the sessions.

Training programs such as those described can apparently affect motivational attitudes, but at the same time training and learning have to be supplemented by doing. Too many fast-track programs have floundered on this. Accelerated promotions for executives with high potential are not successful when they are based solely on training and lack the test of experience.

Even more in error is the training program aimed at obtaining obedience instead of entrepreneurship. One computer company, for example, insists that all new employees take a training course based on programmed instruction. The course book starts out by telling the trainee in several pages how his success will depend on his ability to follow orders with diligence and enthusiasm and without question. Next is an instruction to turn to page ten, skipping the intervening pages. Some trainees of course have curiosity and enterprise sufficient to read the page they were told to skip. When they do they find on it a stern warning that if in the future they fail to obey instructions precisely, they will be severely reprimanded. Sorry, boss. Forgive me, boss.

CHAPTER 5

KEEPING
ENTREPRENEURS
ENTREPRENEURIAL

As outlined in Chapter 4, a number of factors are characteristic of the successful corporate entrepreneur. He survives and even blossoms in a nurturing corporate environment where his needs can be satisfied. He needs to manage people. He needs to achieve as measured by profits, and he has to see the profit figures. He has to be managed loosely from above. He needs broad authority and responsibility over his job and the people who work for him. He needs a job which utilizes his capacity to the full, not an easy or routine job, and not a staff job. And his goals must be reasonable and realistic.

The large corporation's future as a viable organization may well hinge on whether it can create a climate which encourages entrepreneurship and whether its top executives learn to talk about entrepreneurial goals instead of burying projects in red tape and overhead. This can be done only by a marriage of large and small company operational techniques.

A recent survey sponsored by the National Retail Merchants Association found that young executives who worked nights were more satisfied than the ones who worked days and that those in branch stores were happier than those in the main store. Apparently this was due to the greater independence under such conditions. The decrease in direct supervision during night operations and in branch stores apparently increases executive satisfaction.

Managers are made especially unhappy in situations where, in the name of efficiency, the work has been broken down into specializations that are designed to cut down on judgmental demands, on training time, and on the time allowed for making judgments. The trouble is that unspecialized people are hired for these jobs, and they are likely to have many broad skills, some of which will be wasted. And their motivational energy will be sapped by frustration and boredom.

KEEPING THE ENTREPRENEURIAL SPIRIT ALIVE

The small business entrepreneur has psychological advantages over the executive in a large corporation. The small businessman has authority and responsibility, and he leads an exciting life.

H. Ross Perot, the Texan who founded Electronic Data Systems in 1962 on his 32nd birthday after leaving IBM, became a billionaire because he realized the limitations of big organizations. He said: "When you consider the impact that his work has on him and his family, the company has a moral obligation to be an exciting place for an employee."

A substantial percentage of middle- and upper-level big business managers are 35 to 50 years old, an age range characterized by mid-life crises. It is a time of great concern over the state of family or corporate life. Some men fall at this point; others break through to new successes. Psychological researchers have called the last stage of this span of time the "BOOM" (becoming one's own man) period.

It is the frustrated executive, not the successful executive, who has health problems. Humanistic psychologists such as Abraham Maslow and Rollo May have emphasized that two sources of mental health are self-actualization and maintaining a sense of power. In contrast with the older Freudian concept of individual adjustment to the conditions of the environment, the newer psychologists believe in the individual's rising above his environment and doing his own thing. The really healthy person realizes his potentialities, say the humanists. He maintains his power. He takes the risks.

Many a frustrated corporation executive has left his power and benefits behind to start a one-man business of his own. Many another has left and become a management consultant, thus remaining in the same general occupation but on his own, doing his own thing in his own way. Others stay on because they have nowhere to go or they're afraid to go. These executives go on filling their organizational niches, occupying their offices, writing their memos. But their motivation is gone, and with it their productivity.

Little is known about motivation and effective management except that there is a problem and something has to be done about it. One principle that seems to apply is to allow people to stretch bit by bit, to take on more interesting and more responsible work. If managers are allowed to design and define their work, and if they are given a say in establishing the criteria for judging it, there is good reason to think that they will be better managers. An entrepreneurial atmosphere adds something new and exciting to the large company's strength. The job structure can motivate and foster entrepreneurship. But to create such job structures involves psychological and physical considerations.

Such techniques are unconventional, not well known, and

controversial. What is more, they may not work. They are not applicable to all managers under all conditions at all times. Caution in proceeding is advised. These techniques are a radical departure, representing a move away from the scientific management of Frederick Winslow Taylor, which dominated the first half of the twentieth century, and to the humanistic psychology of Maslow, Herzberg, and McGregor.

Some of the effects of low motivation among managers have been listed. Here are other symptoms of the problem:

• Decreasing quality of management
• Casual absenteeism
• High turnover rates (except when other jobs are unavailable)
• Rapidly increasing salaries
• Threats to unionize some lower management levels

The use of carrots and sticks—rewards and punishments—is not enough to control or improve management. Large corporations and their managers will have to come to grips jointly with the psychosocial factors that are at the heart of the problem. The same motivational elements that satisfy the entrepreneur, including authority, accountability, and responsibility, will prove increasingly crucial to management morale and performance. Managers at all levels have to participate in decision making and be measured by profits. Instead of strict supervision, they need freedom. Instead of routine and boredom, they need challenge and the opportunity to make full use of their skills.

People are productive either because being productive fulfills a personal need or because they fear punishment if they don't produce. Fear is a strong short-term motivator. But to be effective over the long term, it must be constantly reinforced, and this makes employees resentful and causes them either to leave or to become malicious.

A University of Michigan study of working people showed that job satisfaction factors ranked in this order: interesting work, enough help and equipment, enough information, enough authority, and good pay. This makes clear that the work ethic is an overwhelming motivational factor—provided that the roadblocks stopping individuals from gaining satisfaction are removed. Money is a decreasing factor in motivation for all employees, but it has never been a prime factor in motivating entrepreneurs. Entrepreneurs do not perform better when they are offered more money; on the contrary, they tend to do worse, because money makes them nervous.

H. G. Van Beek of the department of industrial psychology of the Dutch electronics firm Philips has said: "I wonder if it would be more effective to *give* people more responsibility instead of pointing out repeatedly that they should *feel* more responsible." But many corporation executives are afraid to release responsibility. Abraham Lincoln had no such fear; he delegated great responsibility to his Civil War generals. When a group of influential men came to chide him on this, Lincoln said: "Gentlemen, suppose all the property you were worth were in gold and you had put it in the hands of Blondin to carry across the Niagara River on a rope. Would you shake the cable or keep shouting at him, 'Blondin, stand up a little straighter; Blondin, stoop a little more?' No, you would hold your breath, as well as your tongue, and keep your hands off until he was safely over."

The president of a large company that has had notable success in entrepreneurial new ventures said he believed his company had been successful because its managers "could do anything they wanted, provided it was legal, ethically and morally sound—and proven to be right."

One way of providing redesigned jobs is to break down large organizations into small groups or teams, with each management job enriched through the addition of managerial and control functions. Another possibility is to make sure that all managers set their own goals and measure their own success. That the entrepreneur needs and thrives on this we know for a fact; what we don't know is how much entrepreneurial potential that is now buried in routine and boredom would blossom in such an atmosphere. But the barriers are many. Top management may be negative, for example, or lower management levels may not have the attitudes or skills to become entrepreneurs willing to take on larger and more demanding tasks. . . any case, management should not isolate itself from the contribution that employees at all company levels can make to decisions and actions which lead to profit.

The opening up of communication is the first step in stretching people at all levels to make a contribution, thus increasing involvement and decreasing boredom. Furthermore, open communication between the high and the low will prove beneficial to both. Michael Blumenthal, chairman and president of the giant Bendix Corporation in Southfield, Michigan, said in a *Fortune* interview:

I had thought that the higher up you go, the more sensible the decisions that are made. I found that it ain't necessarily so . . . men in large organizations rely on the quality of the people they choose to work for them. When issues get confused on the way to the top, the chance for wise decisions is less than it might have been at lower levels. I have to remember that I am very dependent on the people below me.[1]

Communication is critical not only from the top down and from the bottom up but between older executives and younger employees. One firm that recognizes this is Levi Strauss &

[1] Quoted in Arthur M. Louis, "The Triple-Threat Man Who Runs Bendix Corporation," *Fortune* (January 1973), pp. 81–85 ff.

Company, whose top executives spend a lot of time listening to young employees because the company's output is sold primarily to young people. All recommendations are turned over to younger staff members for comment and criticism, and the company atmosphere is deliberately informal so that young employees can come to top executives, up to and including the board chairman, with ideas or criticism.

Warning: Job Enrichment May Not Work   According to a survey by David A. Whitsett, a psychological consultant, only one-third of the *Fortune* 500 industrial companies are doing anything beyond the discussion stage about enriching jobs. And in a recent Conference Board survey of 147 companies of various sizes in various industries it was found that 63 companies were using job enrichment, and 10 of these were dissatisfied. The American Management Associations polled 1,093 firms in the summer of 1972, and two-thirds reported improved productivity in the two preceding years; but only 14 percent mentioned using job enrichment programs to stimulate productivity.

There may be only three or four U.S. companies that practice what can truly be called participative management, but there are few successful managements in the United States that do not give their employees more scope and responsibility than they did 20 years ago. The limited and cautious application of the new techniques may be justified. But these techniques do not work for all managers or all employees. Nor do they work in all organizational structures or in all environments. There are a number of indications that perhaps only 15 to 35 percent of employees would today be able to appreciate and benefit from job enrichment.

According to Mitchell Fein, an industrial engineering consultant, only about 15 percent of employees *want* enriched jobs—that is, jobs which are challenging and entail responsibility. It is sometimes difficult to ascertain this by direct survey. Employees may attribute their dissatisfaction to factors other than those that can be improved through job enrichment. Or an employee may rebel against what he believes to be unjust performance standards, not because they are unjust but because he has not been consulted in their creation.

The experience of the humanistic psychologist Abraham Maslow in an academic atmosphere is pertinent here. If anything, the offer of freedom can be more of a shock to a student than to a corporate employee. There are still few hierarchical structures as powerful as a classroom, and the corporate newcomer will be faced with few business procedures as regimented and depersonalized as a multiple-choice examination.

In establishing a psychology department and a graduate program in psychology at Brandeis University when the school opened, Maslow decided to break with tradition and gave the graduate students complete freedom to select their own way of study. Faculty members were consultants only. Maslow related, after ten years of experience with the system, that the approach worked beautifully for about one-third of the students and that these students produced breakthrough theses. For about 42 percent of the students, the results were neutral; they did about the same as they would have under conventional conditions. For the remaining 25 percent of the students, the program was a complete failure. Students in this category were:

1. Passive people who collapsed under freedom
2. Authoritarian personalities who begged to be told what to do
3. Mild psychopaths who regarded the grant of freedom as a sign of staff weakness or foolishness and had fun in trying to sabotage the program
4. Paranoids who could not bear freedom

There are also people who cannot function as managers in such a system:

1. Those who turn it into a hierarchical and bureaucratic system by *imposing* freedom
2. The obsessed who cannot depart from the word of the book
3. Those who have incompatible habits and traditions

At this point, no one knows enough about people or about job enrichment to be able to say what is best for whom and in what circumstances. Perhaps the new approaches should be left to volunteers or tried in experimental situations.

MODIFYING THE ORGANIZATION

Entrepreneurship is difficult to maintain in a large traditional organization. This chapter deals with several ways of modifying the basic vertical pyramidal large company organization to introduce entrepreneurship. Franchising is an old established way that sets up an entrepreneurial organization alongside the conventional corporate form. Other methods of introducing entrepreneurship without undue disturbance to the conventional organization include the new venture team or organization and the corporate spin-off.

More radical changes in organizational structure which aim at making every employee an entrepreneur are discussed in Chapter 7. In this chapter the focus is on the modified traditional forms of organization, variously described as organic, project, product line, program management, matrix, team, group, and venture management. Essentially, such modifications entail setting up teams dedicated to the completion of one goal. These groups are drawn from functional management and remain in existence as long as it takes to complete the task.

THE FRANCHISE ORGANIZATION

A classical way of introducing the entrepreneurial element into the organization is the franchise, in which an independent entrepreneur is linked contractually to a large corporation and given the right to make or sell products of the corporation. For the large corporation, franchises offer many advantages. They represent a diminution of risk, since each franchisee is responsible for his own profit. On the other hand, franchisers have to keep close control over the quality of products and services so as to preserve their reputation in the trade. This is an area which has received much attention and is extensively covered in the literature of franchising.

In 1971 franchised businesses accounted for more than $131 billion in annual sales, or 13 percent of the gross national product and 35 percent of retail sales. The following chart shows that most of the activity is concentrated in a few areas:[2]

Franchise Sales as Percent of Total Sales

Automobile and truck dealers	48%
Gasoline service stations	24
Retailing	12
Fast foods	4
Soft drink bottlers	4
Others	8
Total	100%

THE NEW VENTURE ORGANIZATION

In recent years, the area outside of franchising that has received the most attention with regard to the corporate entrepreneurship aspect is the new venture. New ventures especially require the entrepreneurial skills of the small business. They

[2] See *Franchise Opportunities Handbook.* Washington, D.C.: Government Printing Office (October 1972), pp. 594–598.

are, of course, an area of high risk for both large and small companies. The U.S. Department of Commerce estimates that 60 percent of all new businesses fail during the first two and a half years. There are many reasons: lack of capital, lack of experience, poor management, poor products, poor marketing, and so on. Combining the advantages of large and small companies—for example, large company capital availability and small company flexibility and mobility—can increase the chance of success.

New Ventures in Large Companies   Large companies generally require objective evaluation of ideas for new ventures by formal technoeconomic analysis. Each project must fit the overall long-range plans and objectives of the company. Because the large company has many irons in the fire, as well as many problems with developed businesses, there is a lack of total commitment to any one new venture. In fact, there may even be a lack of commitment to the whole idea of new ventures; acquisition or some other means may be the preferred route to expansion. The large company is often prejudiced against ideas from the outside; it may be said to be suffering from the NIH, or not-invented-here, syndrome. The large company may have no entrepreneurs to run a new venture, or its entrepreneurs may be inhibited and discouraged, especially if their enthusiasm is damped by evaluations that weight risk against cost. Management often prefers to minimize risk by putting the emphasis on extensions of present business, which is understood, rather than venturing into unchartered waters. The strategy for dealing with risk in such a company is simple: bet only on sure things.

In the unlikely event that a new venture *is* launched, the large corporation easily becomes impatient. It may apply strict financial return criteria suitable for its existing businesses, but not suitable to and in the main deadly to the new venture which needs patience as well as money. Corporate hierarchs often penalize personnel involved in failures, not recognizing that there can be no successes if there are no failures.

In a prosperous company it may be hard to find people who would commit themselves wholly to a new product, especially if they have been successful in the past. This is especially true when they continually have to meet rigid financial criteria or when they spend more time in explaining or suffering the consequences of past failures than in developing the product and its markets. No one wants his record smirched because of the failure of a major or even a minor project. As one man put it, "I don't expect that much is going to come of this project. I don't think the company is really going to do anything with these things, but I have a job and I'm going to give them what they ask for, and in four or five years I'll be ready to retire."

Problems plague the new venture throughout its history in the big company. The division of labor among marketing, production, and research hinders coordination. Entrepreneurs are without authority. The corporate no-men are out in full cry, and they can demolish any justification for any new product or any new development. One expert has phrased it this way:

If you have a requirement for superior justification in a company you never can have real progress. There are always good reasons for not doing almost everything. The result is that you send up balloons, watch them rise, and then see whether they are shot down or not. On this basis you try to figure out what will go in your company.

Another problem in the large company is centralization of new ventures in research and development departments, which are technically oriented rather than business oriented and therefore tend to overlook profit. In the small company, the entrepreneur-founder keeps direct control over research. As the company grows, control is divided among a number of functional vice presidents (production, finance, marketing, and others), who interact with the research vice president. If the company becomes a billion-dollar giant, with vice presidents reporting to group vice presidents who report to executive vice presidents, new ventures can become entangled in a snarl of reporting relationships and slowly strangle to death.

In the small company, researchers and managers are thoroughly familiar with day-to-day operations and continually interact. Research deals primarily with process improvement for existing operations or with creating and modifying products in response to customer needs. The projects are small, and they call for small capital expenditures. The objective is a short lead time to profits, results come fast, and the effect on earnings is significant even though the project is small, because the company is also small. In a medium-size company ($100 million in annual sales), which uses research to diversify into new areas, the required investment is larger and the payout longer. For the large company ($1 billion in annual sales), only large projects will do—and, since new products or new markets are risky, the safest project is a new lower-cost process for an established product.

New Ventures in Small Companies   Small new companies have the flexibility to explore a great range of alternatives for new ventures since they have no commitment to established interests. Once they do enter upon a new venture, their commitment to it is total. They are often organized by entrepreneurial individualists with little or no business experience or training who take high risks out of ignorance. They are willing to settle for a small return at the start in the hope that they will find the pot of gold at the end of the rainbow. They react fast to their environment, their financial conditions, and their customer needs.

Their major problem may be lack of capital. The owners' savings and those of their friends are the best source of funds. Financial institutions do not understand them and refuse loans or insist on harsh terms, so a great deal of valuable time is spent in raising money.

As a small new company grows, success brings new problems. The transition from a small new company requires development of broader key management. Fringe benefits have to be added so as to attract qualified men. Costs go up. At a sales level of $5 million a year, profits may level off or decline relative to capital because the large company practices that must be introduced add costs without any commensurate rise in income. In addition, the sales potential of the original product line matures, and new products must be sought for diversification or expansion. What was once a new small company has now become a big company with big problems.

The real advantage of the small company is its entrepreneurial ambience. The atmosphere of a small new company, with its full commitment to a new venture, offers an air of excitement and tension uncharacteristic of the large corporation. Perhaps the factors involved can be illustrated by the early history of Xerox, which depended on commitment.

In 1946 Xerox was a small firm known as the Haloid Company, with sales of almost $7 million and profits that had declined from a $300,000 high in 1939 to $150,000 in 1946. It was at this point that Dr. John Dessauer, director of research, ran across an article in the July 1944 *Radio News* describing a new invention called electrophotography. The inventor was Chester F. Carlson, a patent attorney who had struggled for many years to develop his process of using static electric charges to make dry copies. He had made the first image in 1938, and in 1944 he had interested Battelle Memorial Institute, a nonprofit research institution, in helping financially and technically to carry on the research. In 1946

Haloid became a partner as well. It was 11 years after Carlson's first image before the first Xerox copier was shown. During this period the need for money was critical. John Dessauer even mortgaged his house to help raise money the company so badly needed. When the first automatic Xerox 914 was introduced in 1959, company sales were $33 million a year, four and one-half times the 1946 figure. By 1966, Xerox sales topped $500 million.

Before Carlson sold Battelle on his process in 1944, he had offered rights in the process to every important office equipment company in the country—and was turned down by all. Between 1946 and 1960, Haloid–Xerox spent $75 million on research—twice what it earned. The balance was raised by selling stock and borrowing money.

John Brooks tells of an interview with Dr. Dessauer about the early days. "You want to hear about the old days, eh? Well, it was exciting. It was wonderful. It was also terrible. Sometimes I was going out of my mind, more or less literally. Money was the main problem." While the company was making a modest profit, the cash flow was never enough. Every employee was risking job and career on Carlson's invention. After Dessauer mortgaged his house, his only remaining asset was his life insurance policy. In his words, "Hardly anybody was optimistic. Various members of our group would come in and tell me that the damn thing would never work, and even if it did work, the marketing people thought we were dealing with a potential market of no more than a few thousand machines."[3] Advisers who were called in to evaluate the new product said it would be insane to go ahead with the project. Only in retrospect does it seem to both insiders and outsiders that the project was on the right track and was bound to work out.

[3] "Xerox, Xerox, Xerox, Xerox," in *Business Adventures*. New York: Weybright & Talley (1969), pp. 145–175.

It is noteworthy that despite the outstanding success of Xerox with its office copying machine, it has been less successful in diversifying into other businesses, such as education and computers.

Investment bankers and specialized firms that finance new independent ventures are well aware of the financial risks. In 1968 and 1969, a number of money institutions jumped into the financing of new ventures with undue haste and little study. All that was needed was a short prospectus, an idea, and one or two financial backers to start the ball rolling and attract other investors. Even in the seventies, with principals more sophisticated and investors wary, the chance of success is low. One venture capital specialist estimates that 20 percent of new ventures are successful, 60 percent show mediocre results, and 20 percent are failures.

Experience has shown that the key to success is *good people,* rather than good projects or good prospectuses. If management is really top-notch, a poor project can be kept alive and viable because managers will exert themselves to make things work, find new paths to success, and stay out of trouble. Additional financing to cover errors is hard to get. In venture capital financing, investors want high rewards to compensate them for risks, and they have learned better than to try to salvage a bad deal with good money. This magnifies the effect of setbacks, since available capital is always tight. Investors also want to see that those they finance are committing their own capital, however limited. As one venture capital investor put it, "If a man has $5,000 in the bank, we want to see $4,000 in the venture. If the thing fails, we want it to hurt him more than us."

The Venture Team   Innovation has been called a state of mind, and in a sense venture teams are also a state of mind. A venture team is a new way of approaching an old problem:

successfully launching new business. It consists of a small group of individuals operating within a large company, but simulating small company entrepreneurial qualities. At least that's the concept, but it doesn't always work that way. Unfortunately, many venture teams have been short-lived fads, spending a brief hour in the spotlight and then disappearing quietly. A number of companies that have been acclaimed skillful at new ventures are really failures at it. The source of their publicity is their own public relations departments.

Corporate venture teams were introduced in the early sixties and really caught on in the late sixties. Most large companies have at least experimented with the concept; many are using venture teams under a variety of rules as a standard practice.

The reasons for the interest in new venture teams in large corporations are valid and pressing. Corporate managements recognize that the growth of existing lines has a limit. Sustained profits depend on acquisitions or internal development. Acquisitions may be limited by antitrust considerations or an unattractive price-earnings ratio on the corporate stock. Introducing new products or entering a new business is risky. Moreover, while corporate management is charged with the responsibility for initiating tomorrow's business, it has all it can do to respond to the day-to-day needs and crises of established businesses.

A conventional way of handling new projects is to have them move through existing departments. For example, a new venture might start as an idea in central research and development, move to a commercial development department, then move again, this time to an operating division. At each stage, continuity of personnel and objectives is broken.

In contrast, a venture team stays with the new business from start to maturity. This insures that continuity of personnel and development is preserved, as are common objectives and management. Team members are given a wide range of responsibilities and authority, and the venture team increases the entrepreneurial quotient by (1) streamlining the structure for new venture development, (2) fixing authority and responsibility at the firing line, and (3) creating a climate for innovation.

The successful new venture has to be entrepreneurially oriented and be run by an entrepreneur. Top management is sometimes reluctant to abdicate what it considers to be its prerogatives, but there is no validity for this reluctance. An entrepreneur is a man who has top authority and responsibility on a small scale. He is not a threat to, or a manifestation of weakness in, top management. On the contrary, he is a mechanism for capitalizing on the strength of a business strategy that is applicable to relevant situations. Success in using new venture teams requires not only tolerance of the entrepreneur, but a positive and affirmative action plan to encourage entrepreneurship in the venture.

Getting started is not difficult. Here is a suggested procedure, with the caution that any procedure should be tailored to the company and the environment.

1. *Have top management announce that it is searching for new ventures to be headed up by employee entrepreneurs.* There should not be too many restrictions on the kinds of ventures sought, and those that already exist should be spelled out.

2. *Set up a new ventures or new business development department charged with the responsibility for entrepreneurship.* This department would have seed money to promote limited development and would act as advocate for the new idea. It would also assist in obtaining full funding of the project.

3. *Set up a procedure to review new venture proposals and allocate money to worthwhile ideas.* The process of review

and approval of an idea should not take more than 60 to 90 days.

4. *Set up an adequate compensation scheme,* if one is not already set up. The company's compensation scheme should be changed to reward entrepreneurs for their risks and successes.

Though venture teams were at first mainly a U.S. phenomenon, in the seventies they were being introduced in other countries. For example, in September 1972 Albright & Wilson, a large British chemicals company, announced the establishment of a new ventures division to promote growth outside its present businesses. In forming the new division, David Livingstone, Albright & Wilson's managing director, said:

> The new ventures division will be run by a very small group of people, who will be given a free rein to develop projects for which they see sound and rapid growth prospects. Its structure will be non-bureaucratic, and give every possible encouragement to creative people with entrepreneurial flair.[4]

In establishing this new activity, A&W set two goals:

1. To expand outside of A&W's current business, especially into businesses which show a high return on capital. Projects are to be sought in areas in which A&W has some special strength, technical or commercial, regardless of the industry. Ideas can come from inside or outside the company.

2. To quickly become self-funding and show a high return on capital. "We cannot pour in enormous quantities of money in the hope of a payoff in the future."

Before the new division was established, extensive research was carried out by a team headed up by A&W's planning and development director, Michael Peard. In 1972 the team

---

[4] "A&W Comes Out of Defensive Shell with New Ventures Division," *Chemical Age International* (November 3, 1972), p. 7.

visited eleven U.S. companies, six of which were in the chemicals industry, and seven British companies, five of which were largely in other industries.

The A&W team found that U.S. companies were using new venture approaches characterized by the organization of a new venture management, run on a shoestring initially, and relatively separate from the operating organization. In some cases, new ventures were closely linked to central corporate research and development departments. The study showed that success depended on having a sense of direction, a link to existing businesses, and a great deal of luck. Failure rates were high, especially in the early years, but even one success in six could justify the initial investment. Ten points were found to be crucial to the success of any new venture.

1. *Full support from the top.* Any new venture project that is undertaken with less than full support will be doomed from the start.

2. *A sense of direction.* There should be some sort of fit between the new ventures and the existing businesses.

3. *Clearly spelled out criteria for success.* The people in the venture team should know profit and payback criteria, what funds will be available for the project, and so on.

4. *Patience.* Unusual luck is required for significant profit generation from new ventures within a period shorter than five to eight years. Failure rates during screening and the initial period are high.

5. *Marketing strength.* Technical problems are not normally insuperable. Time and money will overcome most technical difficulties. But marketing strength is critical. Without it and the ability to distinguish interest on the part of a potential customer, a project is likely to fail no matter how technically successful it may be.

6. *Competent personnel.* A venture team has a need for product champions or dedicated project sponsors who will

be able to cut corporate red tape and create confidence in the team and in the project. The entrepreneurial product champion is the key to the success of the project. New product introduction is long, risky, and costly. To provide the commitment that a new product requires takes a particular personality who sees success down the road and is not dissuaded by time, sacrifice, or negative opinions of the experts. If the proponent of the new product often appears to be a crank, he is the crank needed to start up the new venture machinery.

7. *Flexible use of assistance.* The new venture team should be able to obtain assistance when needed and to avoid overcontrol.

8. *Suitable organization style.* Unless the organization is such as to tolerate independence in its venture team, and unless it gives the team responsibility and authority along with accountability, the project will never get off the ground.

9. *Rewards.* Generally, there are no special rewards to new venture personnel other than better salaries, new titles, and psychological rewards. Profit sharing and similar incentives are rare.

10. *Avoidance of fixed ideas.* There should be a willingness to terminate unsuccessful projects or transfer successful projects to interested operating units.

Most people in the game see similar critical points that decide success or failure. According to Herbert E. Engelmeyer, president of Dow Chemical Investment and Finance Corporation, a wholly owned subsidiary of Dow Chemical Company, new venturing has three principal pitfalls:[5] (1) lack of experience in running small businesses; (2) fuzzy thinking about goals and lack of focus on profit and growth criteria; (3) poor projects or overoptimistic project evaluations.

[5] "C&EN Talks with Herbert E. Engelmeyer," *Chemical and Engineering News* (March 19, 1973), p. 16.

In actual practice, three main approaches have been taken to the new venture entrepreneurial organization.

1. Set up a new venture or new enterprise organization which is entrepreneurial in nature and aims at simulating the small company atmosphere in starting up new ventures of very large potential. In such circumstances, success is self-defeating as far as the central venture organization goes. As soon as projects of high potential are identified, attention is focused on such projects. Because they are so large in potential and in cost, effort is concentrated on making them successful and profitable, and the search for further new projects is dropped or deemphasized. Many companies have tried this route, some with significant success.

2. Spin-off new ventures that are small and may be short-changed in a large company structure. The separate companies that are spun off may be partially owned by former employees of the parent, and the parent itself may retain some equity. This is being done by General Electric and others.

3. Set up a venture organization in which the size of the project is not important because the parent company can effectively manage any mix profitably regardless of size and product line. 3M has been notably successful at this.

VENTURE ORGANIZATIONS FOR LARGE PROJECTS

In the late sixties a number of companies set up venture organizations which were devoted to similar objectives, filled needs arising from common problems, and had similar organizations and historical backgrounds. The description that follows is synthesized from the experience of a number of large corporations.

The problem that many organizations shared was the decreasing success of laboratory research in producing profitable commercial products. As a result some companies decided to shift part of their research budget and personnel to a new enterprise or new venture department. This represented a shift from a technical and product orientation to a market orientation.

The typical new enterprise department is charged with exploring paths for corporate growth in areas not properly the province of any of its operating divisions. Although the department is the spearhead of new growth, each separate operating department of the company is charged with growth in its own market areas and for its own product lines. However, the existing divisions have the prime responsibility of earning an acceptable return on their very large investments. This objective prevents the operating divisions from straying far from their existing businesses. The new enterprise department is charged with generating and developing sizable new ventures whose risks are substantial.

One new enterprise vice president described the objective in this way: "We're not interested in lots of new projects— only large ones. We're trying to grow by hundreds of millions of dollars. We want to develop entire new fields, not merely new products." This particular group reached an employment level of 2,000 at one period, corresponding to an annual expenditure rate of $30 million or $40 million a year.

Generally, new enterprise divisions are set up at a high level in the organization and led by a vice president or general manager who reports to the top management level, perhaps the corporation president or the top research and development executive. Thus the top new enterprise man is only a few steps below the chief executive officer. In some cases there is a corporate executive or development committee consisting of top corporate and operating managers as well as the new enterprise executive. The committee's assigned task is to coordinate and expedite all corporate new business development.

Project Organization   Generally, the various projects of the new enterprise department are generated and managed by project managers. These managers have to create new business plans, sell the plans to management, and carry them out, which puts them in an entrepreneurial high-risk, high-reward situation.

The project manager runs a risk because he is in full view of top management and cannot hide his inadequacies and failures. But if he is successful he may end up running a good-size, profitable business.

A project starts when someone in the new enterprise division looks closely at a technological development in the company's research laboratory and decides it can be profitably commercialized. If he can make a case for forming a project, he gets a budget and a time schedule. The sponsor presents his case to management as an action-oriented business plan. It says who will do what when. It also includes the usual financial, market, and venture analyses that are typical of large corporation reports.

If the business plan is accepted, the sponsor becomes project manager and puts together a team of research, engineering, commercial development, and marketing people borrowed from the functional departments. The functional departments back up their team people with professional guidance and help.

The project manager is allowed great freedom of action, no matter what the probability of success. Once the business plan is accepted he can "borrow" corporate money at a stated interest rate. He can buy services from corporate staff or outsiders as he wishes, or rent office space elsewhere if it is cheaper than the available space, or hire full-time staff people from corporate staff departments. The only limits are that he adhere to standard corporate accounting procedures and use corporate lawyers.

Problems of New Enterprise Organizations   There are seven problems which are shared in common by new enterprise organizations:

1. *Finding areas of activity not in conflict with operating divisions or customers.* This is a frequent point of friction within the company.

2. *Identifying and motivating entrepreneurs.* Large corporations have many security-oriented people and many who consider themselves specialists rather than potential managers. Yet hiring outsiders to be enterprise managers has at least two disadvantages: (*a*) they lack familiarity with the organization; (*b*) they disturb the morale of employees who see the plums go to outsiders. Whether the right people are identified in house or brought in from outside, in addition to being entrepreneurs, they have to be able to conform to corporate requirements as well. As one company put it in an advertisement, it was looking for "entrepreneurs who have the ability to conform constructively."

3. *Insuring the laboratory researcher's objectivity.* The laboratory researcher may think he knows more than the commercial people about the commercial potential of his discovery. Yet it is the commercial people who depend on the reactions of potential customers, whereas the laboratory worker can only try to outguess the customer. (This has been termed technical narcissism.) These divergent viewpoints can lead to friction between research and new enterprise personnel unless it is made clear from the start who is responsible for what.

4. *Sustaining top management's commitment.* When top managers are continually involved, they are presold and give what has been termed a creeping commitment, providing funds and support as needed. Creeping commitments help the new enterprise organization. The destructive route is to review the new enterprise only annually or semiannually, when top

management is suddenly exposed to new and unexpected developments without preparation. A marked negative reaction and the sudden termination of the project may result.

5. *Balancing the number and quality of projects.* If too many projects are undertaken, the overall chance of success may increase, but the individual projects will tend to be small, and so will the successes. Alternatively, manpower and money may be spread so thin that nothing much will happen. On the other hand, having too few projects increases the risk of failure, but this risk will be balanced out if the projects are all aggressively manned and completely understood. The best solution is a manageable number of projects of assorted sizes, degrees of risk, and degrees of reward potential—in other words, a balanced portfolio taking into account growth, size, profit, timing, and risk.

6. *Maintaining a balance of commercial and technical considerations to prevent unrewarding research and technical failures.* Both technical and commercial success are desired. This requires a balanced mix of technical and commercial personnel, with power divided between them and with generalists rather than specialists in command.

7. *Having a successful project.* Obviously no new enterprise or new venture operation can go on indefinitely without success as measured by progress and eventual profit operation. According to one new venture manager, one out of three identified projects has to turn into a profitable enterprise with sales in the order of hundreds of millions of dollars before his new venture group will be considered a success by the corporate parent.

New Ventures in the Seventies   The new venture organizations that were formed in the late sixties and survived tended to change in the early seventies. There were two reasons: The first was the business recession that began in 1969, which put pressure on companies to cut costs. The second was the success of new venture organizations in identifying worthwhile projects within their first two to four years of operation.

By 1970 or 1971, many of these organizations turned their attention from finding new projects to developing those they had already found and started down the road to commercialization. Their role and goal were redefined as concentrating on a few major areas of significant promise. Under pressure to reduce costs, corporate managements made significant cuts in research and development budgets, especially in areas outside the main lines of corporate activity. The success of such organizations can be shown by several current examples.

Monsanto Company's New Enterprises Division, formed in 1967, is becoming increasingly active as a pipeline for nontraditional products and services. Products under the wing of this division in 1973 included the well-known AstroTurf; Cerex, a spunbonded nylon fabric; and Spunwire steel fibers, a new reinforcement material for automobile tires. One Monsanto enterprise group became an operating division in mid-1969: Electronic Products and Controls, the first enterprise spun off from the division.

L. Edward "Ned" Klein, the New Enterprise Division's commercial manager, cited an example of the entrepreneurial spirit at work: "When we built the Cerex spunbonded fabric unit, the project managers were so hot to get into production that the plant was built in only five and a half months. It usually takes Monsanto 18 months to build a plant."

W. R. Grace & Co. is another example of success in using the new venture approach. Its corporate technical group developed a Letterflex printing plate system that is an example of a successful business coming out of the venture routine. Letterflex plates are made by polymerization of a plastic, and replace the heavy metal used in printing newspapers. The process was developed at Grace's central research laboratories and turned over to a venture team of young men headed by Gerald Teplitzky, who today is general manager of the Letterflex Division. After several years of development, the process became commercial in 1969; in 1970 the South Bend *Tribune* began using Letterflex plates exclusively. By 1973, 36 newspapers and 12 commercial printers in the United States, Europe, and Japan were using the product.

B. F. Goodrich Chemical Company's procedure has been described by Dr. R. J. Wolf, vice president for development. Once a "go" decision is made on the basis of a preliminary profit analysis of a new project, a business team is set up to commercialize the project. This team is composed of representatives of all the functional groups that can contribute to success. The team is headed by a marketing man and serves in a capacity much like that of the management of a small company.

Dow Chemical Company has established Dow Chemical Investment and Finance Corporation (DCIFC), a wholly owned subsidiary, to finance new ventures. The sole purpose, as stated by Herb Engelmeyer, president of DCIFC, "is to make money." DCIFC figures the minimum investment to make the commitment worthwhile is $250,000. It takes options to buy stock, equity, or a combination of these. Dow is not interested in control or in a permanent investment; its interest is in capital gains. Investments are in lines not directly related to Dow's current operations. New proposals come in at the rate of 40 to 50 a month, of which only two or three are worth in-depth study. By 1973, DCIFC had 18 investments representing $8 million, five made in 1972. The investments cover such varied fields as plasma technology, liquid chromatography, recreational vehicle toilets, semiconductor computer memories, portable oxygen generators, and automatic bag filling and closing equipment.

Scott Paper Company's venture organization combines all the functional specialists into a cohesive group which plans and achieves its business objective. The functional specialties include creative, market research, finance, marketing, research and development, engineering, and manufacturing. Scott Paper's venture management system, based on a set of attitudes toward innovating, includes these two beliefs: "Ideas are a dime a dozen," but people who can develop and commercialize ideas are a rare resource. "The general operating climate must encourage innovation. It is much easier to kill a new idea than to develop one."

New products that are emerging from this development process included Cottonelle bathroom tissue, Job Squad household wiper, QS-12 printing plates, Tanera leather substitute, and the Scott System 200 records storage and management system.

CORPORATE SPIN-OFFS OF NEW VENTURES

Employee groups are buying operations of the large companies they work for, a phenomenon which has become more and more common in recent years. The spin-offs range from underdeveloped new product lines to large subsidiaries which no longer fit the company. One consultant estimates that this accounted for perhaps 5 percent of corporate divestitures in 1972. General Electric has helped form five new companies staffed by former employees and using patents and equipment provided by General Electric. In return, General Electric has received minority stock interests in the companies.

In 1969 Dr. David J. Berdaniel, manager of technical ventures operation, persuaded General Electric to allow company personnel to set up independent companies based on selected technology, with G.E. retaining an equity interest. G.E.'s first such spin-off was Intermagnetics General Corporation of Guilderland, New York, which makes a unique new electromagnet. When it was formed in 1970 it had sales of $500,000 a year and showed a loss. In 1972 sales were about $1 million and some profit was shown. The new Intermagnetics officers raised $60,000 in working capital from their own resources and borrowed $305,000 from a bank, for which they received a 35 percent interest. G.E. holds 46 percent and $150,000 in long-term notes, and a venture capital company received 19 percent in exchange for $200,000 in working capital. A buy-back provision allows General Electric to regain control of the new venture if it should wish to do so.

The other four G.E. spin-offs are Nuclepore Corporation, a producer of a special filter material (some of the venture capital coming from Japan); Ferrodyne Corporation, which makes ferrous diecastings; Community Information Systems, a cable television intercommunications link; and Instructional Industries, Inc., which applies electronic technology for education purposes. Now, General Electric is getting ready to launch four more spin-offs.

In addition, General Electric has used its know-how in a joint venture with a small company, presumably taking advantage of the smaller company's entrepreneurial advantages. Early in 1973 a new company, Integrated Display Systems, Inc., was formed, 60 percent owned by G.E. and 40 percent by Solid State Scientific, Inc., of Montgomeryville, Pennsylvania. Solid State will run the new company under a management contract, even though it has the minority interest. The new company was scheduled to be in production a year after formation to develop and produce timekeeping and automotive devices, using liquid crystal displays and complementary metal oxide semiconductor equipment. Solid State makes equipment into which such devices can be incorporated.

There are a number of advantages for G.E. in its spin-offs and joint ventures:

- It maintains the entrepreneurial spirit despite its large size.
- It uses technologies it cannot otherwise fully exploit.
- It may have the benefit of capital gains.
- It has a window on new markets.
- It has the possibility of buying back successful operations.

Spin-offs involving staff departments have not been notably successful. The usual form in spinning off the computer and data processing department, for example, is to turn the facility into a new company run by former employees. The key employees receive an equity position in the form of stock options or warrants, and the new company is granted a long-term data processing contract from the corporation of which it was once a division. The percentage of ownership is usually related to the contract's duration and its projected or anticipated profitability. The twofold advantage to the corporation lies in the possibility of appreciation of the computer service company's stock and in lower cost as the computer service company increases its size, reduces its overhead in proportion to its total business, and achieves economies of scale.

Unfortunately, most of the experience with such an arrangement has been disappointing. Transforming a group of professionals into entrepreneurs is not always easy or even possible. Often there is no clear understanding of shared objectives and goals when the new company is formed. As a result, misunderstandings crop up later between the new company and the client-owner. Often the capabilities of the new company are overestimated and the marketing, organizational problems, and competition are underestimated. The experience of the service group within the parent may be of little practical value outside the company or industry. Sometimes the service group has developed valuable software and systems which the client-owner is not willing to release to all outsiders. The question of acceptable outside customers becomes a constant point of friction that wastes a great deal of executive time. So do the pricing arrangements between the two companies. As a result the managers of the new company remain involved in company politics in a different way, a way which may be even more complicated and time consuming than it was in the former direct relationship.

In view of the highly competitive atmosphere for computer service companies in the seventies, it is unlikely that such spin-offs will be any more successful in the future. Too many companies in the field are well established and completely independent. To be successful, spin-offs will have to sell highly specialized programs or be situated in geographic areas away from major competitors.

THE MINNESOTA MINING STORY

Most formulas for handling new ventures have one common ingredient: simulating the small business environment and creating entrepreneurial managers. New projects are assigned to men who are given wide authority and responsibility plus the promise of money and status as rewards for success. At the Minnesota Mining & Manufacturing Company (The 3M Company) this philosophy is a way of life that permeates both new and established ventures. 3M Company is a prime testimonial that an entrepreneurial approach can work for a large corporation.

3M is in such products as Scotch brand tape, games, abrasives, dry copiers, and graphic arts products. A *Forbes* article (September 1969) spoke of "little drops of water, little grains of sand" with regard to 3M because its salesmen have a little something for everybody. No single product is truly big in its own right, but together they add up to a real growth company. Few 3M product lines constitute more than 5 percent of sales, and even for the larger items the market is varied and fragmented. No market, no end product is too small to be considered. Just as grains of sand make a beach and drops of water make an ocean, so the almost 40,000 products in the 3M sales line make it an entrepreneurial big company.

There are no junior executive training programs at 3M. Its people are trained for the job on the job. Promotions are from within. Growth is biological; when existing divisions get too fat, they split like fissioning cells and proliferate more fertile cells.

The board of directors at 3M is composed largely of top managers, most of whom have been with the company 25 years or more. Operations are divided into small units. Each division runs much like a separate small company, and each is controlled by budget. The system combines the advantages of big company staff and services with small company mobility. Raymond H. Herzog, 3M's president, describes the management structure as loose. "That doesn't mean we don't watch closely, but we believe in letting people run the show in their own way as long as they bring home results"— meaning an overall 10 percent increase in sales and profits every year. The most important job an executive has is getting top men to work under him. "Get the right people and put them in the proper background with intelligent but loose supervision and you have a winner."

The results have been outstandingly successful. 3M has been averaging a 17 percent return on total capital, and its sales have grown 11 percent per year for the past decade. In 1972, sales topped $2 billion, with products and customers spread over many industries.

Approach to New Ventures   3M Company not only has a New Business Ventures Division, but uses a venture approach to product development at divisional levels as well.

If the originator of a new idea—who could come from research, marketing, manufacturing, or any other function—can convince his supervisor or other appropriate unit of 3M that he has something interesting, he may become a project manager and be allowed to run with the idea. The incentives are money, the chance to prove his idea, and the possibility of becoming a general manager of a new business.

3M encourages the early formation of mini-companies or product teams made up of technical, marketing, production, and financial men recruited, rather than assigned, from other jobs at 3M. If they meet 3M's financial performance criteria, the team members will benefit substantially in status and salary, as well as in the satisfaction each derives from meeting the entrepreneurial challenges of business. If they flop, team members may lose out on several years of normal organizational growth, but will have gained valuable offsetting experience. Entrepreneurs who fail in their own business are likely to lose some of their own capital and would have to look for a job or find the capital for another venture. At 3M they move back into a new job which takes advantage of their entrepreneurial experience, thus allowing them to learn from failure as well as from success.

3M has no minimum size requirements for its new ventures. Opportunities which appear small are not arbitrarily rejected; who can tell where a small idea might lead?

What is unique at 3M is a group of management executives who rose to the top through their own entrepreneurial undertakings. They set the environment, give the idea of an entrepreneurial big company credibility, and motivate would-be entrepreneurs to join and succeed at 3M.

The New Business Ventures Division   At 3M, the New Business Ventures Division has the special charter of working only on projects that are not in the domain of existing divisions. The division has a budget, but no permanent project managers. Employees from any part of 3M may submit new business proposals. Once an idea is accepted, the proposer—or another qualified entrepreneur—is assigned to head the project, given funds for one year, and left free to select his own team. At the end of the year, whether he gets more funds depends on the progress he has made during the year. Progress is more important at this point than potential. He gets the money because he has shown capability and tangible achievements. The *man* gets the money, not the project. Three factors operate to make the system successful: (1) It has worked notably well for many years. (2) Men whose projects fail are not labeled failures; they are considered lucky to have had a rare chance, and they return to other positions at 3M. (3) The budgetary system rewards results, not potential.

An Entrepreneurial Atmosphere   From the top of 3M down, key executives encourage entrepreneurial behavior by their own personal example, by vocal encouragement, and by devoting significant corporate resources to the principle. Any individual is free to seek encouragement and capital support for his idea from any part of the company. President Herzog comments:

The practice is based on the theory that only 5 to 10 percent of the employees are bound to be leaders and you find these by giving them their head. We set no limits on areas we get into, but we do not invest massively at the beginning in anything. We look for a toehold in an evolving area and move in gradually as we increase both our technical competence and market understanding.[6]

Far from insisting on a quick return from a new product, 3M is willing to look at red figures for a few years. Eventually the new product will be expected to show at least a 10 percent

[6] Quoted in William D. Smith, "Former Basketball Coach Now Leading 3M Varsity," *New York Times* (November 8, 1970).

sales gain per year and an 18 to 20 percent return on total capital. 3M has patience. Bert Cross, who was 3M's president in the sixties, came up through the development route. "I've been there myself," he once said. "I know how it feels, and I don't lose patience with them. I don't cut a guy off. He knows more than you about that product and its market. If he doesn't, then the question you should ask is why he is there in the first place." Harry Heltzer, now chairman of the board and chief executive officer of 3M, has emphasized that people—*not* dollars—develop new products. Dollars only help. In deciding whether to continue a project, a great deal of weight is given to the attitude and determination of the project leader. Chairman Heltzer says: "Not so many years ago some of the leading scientists at my company were thought to be extremely stubborn . . . they were . . . they fought . . . they stuck." He concludes: "Until you succeed you're stubborn—when you succeed you're persistent."

CHAPTER 6

KEEPING THE ACQUIRED ENTREPRENEUR

THE ENTREPRENEUR who has built his own company from scratch is wined, dined, and courted by the large corporation until he agrees to be acquired. But once the acquisition is completed and the honeymoon is over, severe conflict becomes the order of the day. The acquisition was probably negotiated by staff members of an acquisition department who disappear once the acquisition is consummated. Then the entrepreneur may be put under the authority of a top executive who comes from a different socioeconomic background and has a different life-style and different business philosophy.

WHAT DO YOU DO WHEN THE HONEYMOON IS OVER?

Whether—and how—to fit the newly acquired entrepreneur into the large corporate atmosphere is critical to both the acquired and acquirer. Sources of conflict are many. The new situation may not suit the entrepreneur or fit his abilities. It may not satisfy the achievement needs and other drives which made him an entrepreneur. He may feel restrained in his ambitions and caught in an endless round of reporting that has nothing to do with his operation. Perhaps he is made to feel like a little pea in a big pot of soup. He is surrounded by bigger powers. He is expected to give up much of the power he generated with his own resources. Requests for decisions have to go up and down several layers of management. Visitors from headquarters continually invade his office and plant. His winers and diners are transmuted into naggers and complainers. His life and soul are no longer his own. But he is probably a millionaire now, and if he doesn't like the situation he can take his money and go.

Some companies appear to have avoided major problems. One such company, National Service Industries, is literally an association of friends and relatives. It is an Atlanta-based conglomerate of the most miscellaneous sort: men's shirts, dinette furniture, lighting fixtures, work gloves, envelopes, rental furniture, rental towels and sheets, sanitation products. Sales are about $400 million a year. The record shows continuing increase in earnings, a return of 20 percent on equity, and less than 10 percent debt. The president is Erwin Zaban, 51, who dropped out of high school when he was 15 to help in his father's struggling janitorial supplies business. It was successful and became Zep Manufacturing Company.

National Service Industries was formed by a merger of friends and neighbors who knew each other socially or through business or both. All were well known in Atlanta's Jewish community. The cornerstones of the company were Erwin Zaban's Zep Manufacturing Company, Erwin and Milton Weinstein's National Linen Service Corporation, David Goldwasser's envelope company, Freeman's lighting company, and Selig Chemicals.

When Erwin Zaban ran out of friends to acquire, he followed the same principles as before in considering new acquisitions: could the new management fit in with the old? "Sometimes when we're negotiating to take over a company, I just get the feeling that this guy isn't going to fit into our group. When I get this feeling, we call off the whole deal."

The personal touch in management is acknowledged to be important. Talking about a recent acquisition, Zaban said:

> It was a family business, but doing very well. So, instead of imposing a management chart on them, we interviewed everybody in the business, found out what they did, and made up a chart that reflected the actual situation. We don't want ever to kill the entrepreneurial spirit.

Just as the entrepreneur has his problems with the corporation, the corporation has its problems with him. He is not used to taking orders or giving a close account of his business actions, and he is used to dealing strongly and authoritatively with subordinates.

As his company grows and the entrepreneur finds it too much for one man to handle, he may nevertheless be unwilling to yield control. When participative or consultative management techniques are indicated, and he knows it, he may be unable to yield authority. Such a man is unsuited by temperament and ability to manage a large unit of a large company. Or perhaps he was successful because he was lucky rather than skillful. In that event, sooner or later his lack of ability is bound to become evident, and it will become clear that he cannot perform.

U.S. INDUSTRIES, INC.

U.S. Industries, Inc. (USI)* is a conglomerate that has grown in about a dozen years from $88 million to more than

---

* This section on USI is based on articles from *Forbes* (August 1970, November 1972), *Financial World* (August 1969, October 1970, September 1972), *Dow Digest* (September 1972), *Value Line* (March 1973), *Plastics World* (February 1970), *Daily News Record* (August 1969), and *Advertising Age* (March 1970).

$1.5 billion in annual sales. In the seven-year period from 1966 through 1972, 124 medium-size firms were acquired, not one of them accounting for more than 5 percent of profits. The company sells a wide variety of products: apparel and accessories (26 percent of sales); industrial and agribusiness equipment (23 percent of sales); building materials, construction, shelter, and furnishings (35 percent of sales); and health and leisure products and services (16 percent of sales).

USI attributes its rapid growth to a joining of the entrepreneurial spirit and growth potential of small, successful companies in fragmented industries to the financial and managerial advantages of a larger corporation. Original management is retained in all cases and given help in financing, marketing, manufacturing, and other areas whenever useful. Financial controls are thorough, but each operation is independent in all other respects. Contingent payouts are used in most acquisitions as incentives for growth, but few divisional presidents have left after earning their contingencies.

Original managements must agree to stay when their companies are acquired since they are usually best qualified to maintain growth. Emphasis has been on small companies because they have greater potential for growth and they provide a way to spread the risk. Fragmented industries where USI can grow into a major factor have been favored.

The philosophy of U.S. Industries (as quoted from its 1972 Annual Report) is summed up in this creed:

Our basic business is helping small companies grow. Small companies are the heart of USI. In helping them grow, USI insures its own growth. . . .

Our experience over the past seven years suggests that small companies—run by people who use business as a means of expressing a personal creativity and search for improvement—are most responsive to the needs of a changing world.

The average acquisition candidate runs about $10 million to

$20 million a year in sales. The growth and profit pattern
is shown in Table 1.

TABLE 1. U.S. Industries, financial data in summary.

	TOTAL		PER SHARE		PERCENT EARNED ON TOTAL CAPITAL
YEAR	SALES ($ MILLION)	NET INCOME/ (LOSS) ($ MILLION)	SALES (DOL- LARS)	NET INCOME/ (LOSS) (DOLLARS)	
1960	$ 88	$(0.3)	$18	$(0.07)	1
1965	126	6.3	25	1.18	17
1970	1,232	65.8	54	2.64	14
1971	1,407	72.7	51	2.44	13
1972	1,579	77.4	52	2.50	N.A.

SOURCE: *Value Line* (March 9, 1973) p. 1256.
N.A.: not available.

While progress has been slowed by the recession of 1969–
1972 as well as by a general disenchantment with conglomerates, USI has performed well relative to the economy and
to other conglomerates. And it continues to make acquisitions,
as shown in Table 2.

TABLE 2. U.S. Industries, acquisitions.

YEARS	NUMBER OF COMPANIES ACQUIRED
1966, 1967	17
1968	36
1969	53
1970	4
1971	8
1972	6
Total	124

Acquisition Criteria   Part of the success of USI may be attributed to strict acquisition criteria, including the following seven:

1. Sales of $10 million to $30 million a year
2. Pretax net profit of $1 million or more; 20 percent or more pretax return on total capital
3. Well and aggressively managed by an entrepreneur rather than a professional manager
4. Evidence of internal growth and potential for continued growth; internal growth of at least 15 percent a year in the preceding three or four years
5. Management agreement to stay on in control after acquisition
6. Management agreement to follow USI's uniform accounting system
7. At least potential management talent at lower levels, because many of the acquired companies are relatively small one-man organizations

USI prefers to acquire medium-size companies with $10 million to $30 million a year in sales so as to avoid antitrust problems, insure greater growth potential, and prevent overdependence on a single earnings source. On the other hand, it avoids smaller companies (sales under $10 million a year) because they often don't know where they are going, have not demonstrated durability, and are still one-man shows with no actual or potential second level of management.

Motives and Incentives for Acquired Companies   Why entrepreneurs merge into USI may best be illustrated by a case history. USI has subdivided its acquired companies into several groups. One of these is the plastics and chemicals group, made up of some half a dozen acquired companies.

The first plastics company acquisition was Leon Chemical

& Plastics. Leon, founded and developed by Arthur Nicholas, specialized in seatbelt components made by dip-molding of polyvinyl chloride. With the greatly increased use of seatbelts (80 million in 1969 as against 100,000 in 1960), Leon had to expand facilities and went in search of outside capital, a common occurrence among successful small companies. Banks were willing to lend the money, but made certain restrictive demands that Mr. Nicholas was unwilling to accept. He was therefore receptive to USI's acquisition offer. USI provided the capital for expansion and Mr. Nicholas received a large down payment, with the balance contingent upon a doubling of profits in five years. Profits tripled the first year, and Mr. Nicholas ended up with $3 million in USI stock. Here is his story:

He was 29 years old, earning about $15,000 a year, and expecting a first child. The day after his wife broke the news of a baby on the way, Arthur Nicholas figured it was "now or never," and quit his job as a chemical engineer. He started Leon Chemical & Plastics, but had nothing to sell. Finally, he developed a household cleaner, and invested two or three hundred dollars in it. In two years, Leon had sales of $100,000, and broke even. Nicholas' salary was at the poverty level. Then, in 1962, he read a study on seatbelts. Only about 10,000 pairs were in use. He bought a set and worked on ways to improve them through plastics. One of his patents is so basic that practically all seatbelts are using it. There are about 70 million seatbelts installed in automobiles every year, most of them with a part made by Leon Chemical.

But Leon Chemical was growing too fast, and needed money to expand. They either had to sell or go public. USI made a good offer. Suddenly the company became theirs. Nicholas waited for orders that never came. He kept running his own company in the same way he always had. This was important to an entrepreneur like Nicholas who wanted independence. He had always wanted to be a millionaire, and he became one. But he was even prouder of having built up a company employing several hundred people.

Nicholas mentioned some of the benefits offered by merger with USI, including the obvious one: money. The USI family includes 40 or 50 millionaires serving as company presidents and group chairmen. And there are further incentives which keep entrepreneurs happy and active.

Units benefit from the availability of capital as well as from technical and other interaction between operating units. USI keeps its entrepreneurs concentrated on making and selling the products of their units. Centralized managerial support is given in staff areas: legal, tax, insurance, and labor relations. There is a program of motivation and development: financial rewards, advancement to group levels, and broader responsibilities. Contributing to a winning team is also a kind of motivation. Operating and staff management people come from a wide mixture of ethnic, socioeconomic, religious, and educational backgrounds, which minimizes conflict or friction from these sources.

Max L. Cohen, founder and president of Mr. Dino, a division of USI, stayed on after his firm was acquired because he loved his business and he loved the continuance of the competitive spirit at USI. He had thought that the great amount of money he had made might cause him to relax. It did not. It was not only his egotism and drive that kept him going but the friendly competition with the other 27 entrepreneurs heading companies in USI's apparel group. Most of them were millionaires, some multimillionaires. Max Cohen said of these apparel group company presidents: ". . . you'd think we were still out trying to make our first dollar."

Management and Control   USI chairman I. John Billera and his small headquarters staff make no pretense of running all the businesses that make up the corporation. They keep on the old management and confine themselves to auditing the results and controlling the cash flow. There is a monthly review by group chairmen, no one of whom has more than eight companies under his control. Billera says USI doesn't "indulge in the sins of synergy. We have 126 accounting departments and 126 purchasing departments. This is waste. But we're trying to perpetuate small company dynamics."

USI seeks to maintain the environment through management by objectives, as distinguished from management by directives. The key is to have all basic corporate objectives understood by the entire management group. These objectives are planned and recommended by the corporate planning group for the approval of the chairman, the president, and the board of directors. Objectives are reviewed and discussed, and progress toward them is measured at the annual presidents' council. This is a meeting of all headquarters and group office executives and division presidents, with a second representative from each division on a rotating basis. These same executives meet in separate group presidents' councils once each quarter for a more detailed appraisal of the progress each operation is making against overall objectives and against individual division budgets, which are prepared annually. At each division, progress is reviewed monthly at executive committee meetings.

With corporate objectives and guidelines well understood, and with individual budgets formulated, each division is free to pursue its goals in the manner which brought it earlier success. There is no overburden of headquarters-devised procedures to inhibit men who have found their own way to be successful.

A system of frequent direct communication, oral and written, promotes quick response to deviations from budgets or objectives as well as to problems and opportunities. Each company sends in a monthly report showing actual against budgeted profits. Deadlines are rigid, and units which meet goals are not interfered with.

Why USI Works   The foregoing description has touched on some of the factors that have led to USI's success. But there are other important factors, including a high degree of profit orientation at the corporate level. When John Billera took over the management in 1965 and the company set out on its intensive acquisition program, he said USI is in business "to make profits, not products."

Another important success factor is a general spirit of entrepreneurial philosophy permeating the company. More than 40 percent of USI's stock is held by managers who came with their acquired companies. The stockholders thus own and manage USI, and the interests of owners and managers are merged, not separated as they are in most large corporations.

Perhaps John Billera is especially sympathetic to entrepreneurs because he was once himself brushed aside in a corporate takeover. With two other men he went into a small packaging firm at half pay in hopes of eventually having a piece of it. They had moved the company from the red to the black side of the ledger when it was sold. The new owner asked Billera, who had been chief financial officer, if he wanted to be assistant treasurer. "I told him to shove off." Billera has built a big complex without killing the entrepreneurial spirit of his small acquisitions. This is a rare company.

GIVING ENTREPRENEURS NEW WORLDS TO CONQUER

One of the key problems of entrepreneurs and of many managers is that they cannot grow with their company. After it passes a certain size, they no longer have the desire or the competence to go on running it. Or perhaps they are underutilized, as is the case when market limitations put a limit on the growth of their company. The true entrepreneur can't stay idle, even part of the time.

In the case of the entrepreneur who can't grow with his company, it may be possible to reposition him in a fledgling business. If he is most effective in running something very small and very new, it is a mistake to assign him to staff work, for which he is unsuited and which can only make him unhappy. The entrepreneur flourishes in a profit environment. He needs new and bigger worlds to conquer. He doesn't want to relax and enjoy his new-found millions; he wants to work.

ACQUIRING ENTREPRENEURS DOESN'T ALWAYS WORK

Despite the best intentions, it is not always easy to keep the entrepreneur happy. In some cases the nature of the industry militates against successful collaboration between the acquirer and the acquired. It has been said that the construction industry falls into this category, especially in the area of residential construction. The failure to recognize the local nature of the building industry has been a major factor in the unhappy relations between builders and the large corporations that have acquired them. What the corporate parents did not understand is that operational decisions have to be made at the local level.

Thinking big is wrong for the building business. U.S. Home is probably the largest builder in the country, and it has succeeded because it is a combination of 22 builders, each doing his thing. U.S. Home expects each of the 22 builders under its umbrella to make money in his own neighborhood. Each can effectively compete locally against the small local builder because each is small. But together they're big.

At least one large conglomerate ran into problems with an acquired construction company. At the time of acquisition, the entrepreneur primarily responsible for the success of his construction company was near retirement. He had had differences with his son, who had left to set up his own company. However, the second management level had not been neglected. When the founder retired, two promising men, both relatively young and both highly entrepreneurially oriented, took over as president and executive vice president.

The new president, 41 years old, had been employed by the acquired construction company for ten years. He had been orphaned while still in college, and at age 20 he took over the family shoe business, continuing with his college education at night. At 24 he joined a real estate venture group, was very successful, and later went to work for the construction company. Here he found a group of executives most of whom had once been independent builders and professionals, "the kind you'd never dream you could get into a corporation and teach corporate manners."

The new executive vice president for operations was 38 at the time of the merger. He had headed his own building firm before joining the construction firm eight years previously.

After the merger, everything seemed to go well at first. But two years later, after many months of friction, the two top men quit. According to press reports, executives of the construction subsidiary believed there was a basic incompatibility between a construction-oriented company and one grounded in traditional industrial practices. Construction industry executives used phrases such as "conflicting life-styles" and "different ways of doing things" when discussing the subsidiary and its parent.

Acquired entrepreneurs do not always stay, and their departure leaves the corporate parent with the task of selecting a replacement. If the acquired company is still small, the entrepreneurial factor must be taken into account, in terms both of people and of management techniques.

One large company lost the management team of a small acquisition about a year after the merger when the former owners lost interest. The acquisition is now being successfully run by a 55-year-old company executive with broad experience. This change in management has succeeded because the parent treats the acquisition like the small entrepreneurial company it is. The parent company plays the role of banker and leaves the president of the subsidiary with complete authority. The products and business of the subsidiary are substantially different from those of the parent, and the parent recognizes that it can contribute little but capital and management help. The subsidiary is not arbitrarily loaded with corporate overheads such as legal and financial charges; it pays only for what it uses and is free to seek the same services elsewhere if it can get equivalent quality at lower cost.

In contrast, a large conglomerate bought a small pot-and-kettle chemicals company which had been quite profitable. The conglomerate's central engineering department then surveyed the plant and recommended building a new plant and installing a new continuous process to cut costs. The founder and owner of the acquisition wrote several letters to the conglomerate's president challenging the value of the new process and pointing out the risk. The corporate engineers won, the new plant was built, and it was a disaster. Luckily, the old pot-and-kettle plant survived and continued to produce. Why did such an episode occur? Because conglomerate officers couldn't believe that the founder-entrepreneur could be smarter about plant design than their staff of skilled engineers. They learned an expensive lesson.

MOTIVATING MILLIONAIRES

It is generally beneficial for the acquirer to keep the entrepreneur and for the entrepreneur to stay. Usually each needs the other. One of the key factors in an acquisition is the quality of the acquired company's management and personnel and their compatibility with the personnel of the acquirer. Even large conglomerates rarely have a surplus of qualified management personnel who can act as replacements should the acquired management not perform satisfactorily. On the contrary, in actual practice many managers have found themselves able to move up to top positions in the parent company after their units have been acquired. This has been as true of medium-size companies like Witco Chemical as of large conglomerates like W. R. Grace & Co.

What motivates the entrepreneur to stay with the big corporation? Several things. He has become a stockholder and can benefit by stock appreciation. He can get bonuses. He may have retained an interest of some sort in his own subsidiary's profits. Part of the payment he receives may be tied to the profits he can generate after the deal goes through. The merger has solved some of his estate and tax problems. He has gone public by becoming part of an already public company—a method that is far less costly and time consuming than launching a new issue of stock would have been. But his stock makes him an owner of his new corporate parent, and what helps the parent helps him.

By this time, the entrepreneur may be a millionaire. Questions are spinning around in his head. The first days or months after the acquisition may be critical to success. The new millionaire is thinking, as suggested by Gerald Katz:[1]

- Will I get the capital I need to expand?
- Will I be able to work for a loss?
- Will I have to get approval for every decision?

[1] "How to Motivate a Millionaire," paper presented to Chemical Marketing Research Association, September 1971.

- What will happen to my organization? Will there be massive layoffs, demotions?
- Will my plans be carried out? Will I be consulted on the future of my unit?
- Will I have to move to another city?
- Will I and other key personnel have a chance to grow in the new organization? Be of use? Get a chance to try for top management in the parent?
- Is the stock of the parent company which I am getting for my company a good one in terms of yield and appreciation?
- Will I be able to discuss my problems easily with and have access to top parent company officers? At what level will I report?
- Will I benefit by good staff support: financial, legal, engineering, safety, insurance without too heavy overhead charges?
- What if our benefits are better than the parent's—will our benefits be reduced? If theirs are better, will we get them?

The president of one large company follows the final signing of merger papers with a first-class dinner at which he again spells out to the acquired entrepreneurs his philosophy of operation and the fact that he is easily accessible to hear their problems by phone or personally.

KEEPING THE ACQUIRED ENTREPRENEUR WILL BE MORE IMPORTANT

The problem of keeping acquired entrepreneurs will be more important in the future than it ever has been because of the increasing importance of small company acquisition as an expansion route.

The day of the big merger deal is over for the time being, for a number of reasons: antitrust actions, changes in accounting procedures for acquisitions, declines in stock prices of conglomerates. Corporations interested in acquisitions will therefore be doing more looking at smaller companies that are still being run by their entrepreneurial founders. As these men get older, estate problems make ownership of a widely held public stock attractive. Most of them own companies that are too small to go public, or they find new issue conditions unattractive. The situation is especially critical where there are no more family members interested in taking over the business. From the viewpoint of society, it is also desirable that there be a marketplace for small firms, when entrepreneurs have no other way to get the return they struggled so hard to realize.

CHAPTER 7

CORPORATE ORGANIZATION AND ENTREPRENEURSHIP

EARLIER pages contrasted the entrepreneur and the hierarch, the small business and the large corporate bureaucracy, and they detailed some of the ways in which the traditional organization has been modified to allow some scope for entrepreneurship. The pages that follow focus on the historical development of radically new organizational structures whose aim is to make every employee an entrepreneur.

The philosopher Hegel postulated what has come to be known as the Hegelian dialectic, which describes any process of development. There are two inseparable aspects: (1) the emergence of something new and (2) the discarding of the old. In every new development are the seeds for its own destruction, out of which a new order arises. Hegel gave the steps in development the labels thesis, antithesis, synthesis, and said that every synthesis in turn becomes the thesis for the next cycle of development.

If thesis characterizes the entrepreneur and the small business, and antithesis characterizes the hierarch and the corporate bureaucracy, what will the characteristics of the new synthesis be? Clearly a change is coming in business organization which will synthesize elements of the small and large.

THE NEW ORGANIZATION

In the new organization—tomorrow's organization—the large corporation will consist of relatively small groups or teams that are profit centers with a great deal of autonomy, responsibility, and authority. The principal function of the central management will be directing the flow of capital to areas where it will earn the highest return, as defined by the need to please stockholders through dividends and stock appreciation. Groups and teams not only will be operating units but will have a great deal to say about planning and controls and will participate with central management in setting goals and in measuring success.

Such an organization will bring entrepreneurship into the large corporation. It will also increase flexibility by shortening the lines of communication and increasing the number of communication paths. Teams will communicate directly with central management, as well as with other small groups at any level.

Actually, a great deal of this is already going on, even though it is not recognized on formal organization charts. For this reason many organizations that look unwieldy on paper function very effectively through informal channels. This serves to confuse outsiders and newcomers who are unaware of the informal communication channels. But it is a truism that practice leads theory and formality in organization.

The traditional organizational form has been variously described as functional, line-staff, pyramidal, mechanistic, hierarchical, authoritarian, bureaucratic, and German-general-staff. New and modified forms have been given such names as organic, project, product line, program management, matrix, team, group, or venture management organization. Perhaps the new synthesis requires a catchy name to make it popular. When Dr. H. C. Wechsler was president of the Borden Chemical Company, he used the term "reticulated company" to designate a netlike organizational structure. Collegial organization and adhocracy are other semantic possibilities.

In an organization with real teamwork, members think about "our" problems because they identify with the company and its problems. They feel free to challenge the opinions of superiors and peers without fear of losing their jobs or their chances for promotion. Members of the team can express themselves and thus be involved in a meaningful and creative way. This kind of atmosphere brings the team members closer to the profit goal and appeals to the young entrepreneurial people who will be needed in future years.

In many companies, information feeds in only one direction: up. There is no feedback to the lower levels where it is needed for self-evaluation and self-improvement. But not in the new organization. The top executive of such an organization will have to understand behavioral dynamics—intergroup and intragroup relations, motivation, and interpersonal relations. And he will have to be responsible for intergroup communications and access to the information flow.

Organizations take one of three fundamental shapes: vertical, horizontal, or reticulated.

THE VERTICAL ORGANIZATION

The vertical organization is diagrammed in Figure 2. The letters represent individuals; the lines, organizational links. In the vertical organization these links are as emotional as esprit de corps. The vertical organization is made up of a group

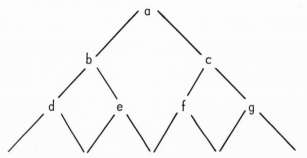

Figure 2. Vertical organizational structure.

of people who share a situational position or frame, as, for example, all those living in a specific defined area or all those working for a certain company. The members of the group have different attributes—that is, different individual characteristics, which may be inherent (age, hereditary traits) or acquired (education, social status, occupation). Whereas a group with common attributes is cohesive because of its homogeneity, a heterogeneous group based on a frame requires the addition of a unifying factor or factors to attain cohesiveness. Such unifying factors include (1) a "sense of unity" or esprit de corps and (2) an internal organization. These two factors are interrelated, each supporting the other. A sense of unity is emotional or psychological, involving close contact between the individuals of the group to infuse them with the feeling of belonging. Military uniforms are a unifying factor, as are the white shirts worn by IBM employees.

Heterogeneous frame organizations are always vertical. Examples are the relations of parent to child and those of superior to subordinate. In vertical organizations, there is a strong consciousness of rank.

The vertical structure has these four characteristics: (1) It is usually difficult to change the leader. (2) There can never be more than one leader. (3) Only one person can be in a position at any one time. (4) Control has to be exercised through intermediaries. This is why the strength of overall control can never be greater than the strength of the weakest link.

Weaknesses of the vertical structure include the following: (1) Loss of the leader stirs up great internal stress. (2) The organization is highly affected by emotional personal relationships. (3) As the group grows, the leader's control over individual members dwindles as the distance between them increases. (4) Superior-subordinate relationships become largely power struggles for the superior positions rather than a means for getting the work done. (5) Because of rank privileges and consciousness, factors other than ability play a large part in promotion and position. (6) Self-development is restricted and job dissatisfaction is widespread. Breakdowns in the vertical structure result in factionalism.

Advantages of the vertical organization are threefold. (1) It enables the leader to communicate swiftly with every member, even on the lowest level. (2) It is highly effective at mobilizing members. (3) It has the ability to make quick major decisions when necessary, through the hierarchical power structure. However, members on the lower levels of the hierarchy find it slow to arrive at less important decisions affecting them because the decision-making process entails the movement of information up and down several management layers.

A tight vertical organization can be a wonderful machine. The links holding the organization together, such as esprit de corps, are more important than the individuals in the organization. The system will tolerate mediocrity in its members as long as they maintain communication and relate properly to superiors and subordinates. This lends itself especially to military organizations. A cynic once characterized the U.S. Navy as an organization conceived by geniuses for operation by idiots. However, with a rise in individualism and nonconformism even military organizations are having problems of an organizational nature.

Admiral Hyman Rickover, mentioned earlier as a military entrepreneur, was firm in his belief that the first rule for success is to build a staff of motivated and intelligent people, and he was highly selective. But Admiral Elmo Zumwalt, the top commander in the Navy in 1973, isn't able to be as selective. Admiral Zumwalt has to achieve a successful working organization with *all* the people in the Navy. He needs new approaches to meet new attitudes. In 1972, 130 Navy men refused to rejoin the aircraft carrier *Constellation* and were reassigned to other stations. A few years before they would have been jailed as mutineers.

The story is told of a World War I private who left his squad in the middle of a battle, but came back with a dozen German prisoners. His sergeant berated him for going AWOL yet had to admit that the private was a hero. "But why did you do it?" he asked the private. "I wanted to go into business for myself," replied the private. Similarly, in what *New York Times* reporter Neil Sheehan called *The Arnheiter Affair,* a U.S. Navy officer took his ship into combat zone and engaged the enemy contrary to orders. Both are demonstrations of entrepreneurship, which, with rare exceptions, is not tolerable *within* the vertical organization.

The management of military organizations has to change. Modern military technology, *Fortune* editor Max Ways has pointed out, can no longer be handled by robots of the Frederick-the-Great design. Even in the most authoritarian vertical organizations, discipline has been weakened. Max Ways cited a disgruntled football player who complained about his club's "antiquated management" with its "Mickey Mouse" rules, and said that the new college graduates entering football would not stand for this. As a matter of fact, the managements of most football clubs have begun to relax their control of players, not primarily because players' attitudes have changed but because the game of football, as now played, requires participants who are capable of initiative and self-discipline.

The leader in the vertical structure can exert his power over most of the members only indirectly, through his immediate subordinates. Thus his subordinates also have great power. Since each is the representative of his own subordinates and their interests, the leader must insure a balance of power among his subordinates. And, since the leader's source of power is his subordinates, he must be ready to accept their views and comply with their wishes.

In the vertical relationship, superior and subordinate do not benefit each other equally. Protection is paid for with dependence, and affection with loyalty. This means emotional relationships stronger than those in horizontal organizations, which are based on groupings of persons with common attributes.

However, a vertical organization as an *entirety* can be highly entrepreneurial and effective in the growth and development of new ventures despite the nature and composition of its individual components. There are many evidences of this, but the best overall examples are the Japanese companies which are not only completely vertical, but extremely entrepreneurial as well, both singly and in combination with the other elements of Japanese industry.

THE HORIZONTAL ORGANIZATION

The horizontal organization is diagrammed in Figure 3. The letters represent individuals; the lines, organizational links. In the horizontal organization the links are based on the common attributes and common interests of the individuals. Horizontal organizations are based on the sharing of those common attributes: education, social status, occupation.

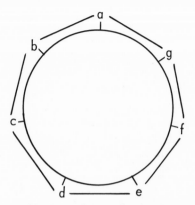

Figure 3. Horizontal organizational structure.

Among the groups with common attributes are occupational groups, families, and castes. A horizontal relationship is brother to brother or colleague to colleague; a strong sense of fellowship is the source of solidarity, and consciousness of rank is extremely weak. Professionals—doctors, chemists, accountants, consultants—tend to organize in a horizontal way.

Horizontal organizations have two disadvantages: (1) difficulty of communication in a vertical direction and (2) difficulty of administering tasks requiring a variety of skills.

A horizontally organized team is a group of people who manage themselves. This form of organization satisfies the need to belong to a group and to get response from people one is close to or interested in and whose approval and support are desired. The members of the group spend many hours together—possibly more than with relatives or friends outside the group. They are highly motivated to act in accord with group goals and values so as to obtain recognition, support, security, and praise.

In horizontal organizations, movement is not up some ladder, but is fluid and more lateral. People can come and go more or less freely. In a vertical organization it would be difficult for a man to take months off for other duties or for a sabbatical, whereas in a horizontal organization he could move in and out. An executive could take two years off to be an ambassador or run a special commission, without having to worry about what the competition was up to while he was away. It is in the vertical organization that the race is to move up to the top. Not so in the horizontal organization. What is more, retirement is eased. The employee in the horizontal group can easily withdraw without undue upset to the organization as a whole.

THE RETICULATED, OR MATRIX, ORGANIZATION

In the reticulated organization, vertical and horizontal groupings are combined. Small groups of individuals interrelate with one another, and the groups are interconnected in a matrix or network.

Within the groups, the individuals are held together by common attributes and goals, and they tend to be similar. The groups themselves are connected with other groups through contractual instead of personal relations. The term *contractual* refers to an agreement as to common goals and objectives. Contractual arrangements are an old Anglo-Saxon custom; the Mayflower Compact of 1620 was such an agreement among the Pilgrims. The reticulated organization is diagrammed in Figure 4. The letters represent small groups of individuals in a horizontal organization. The lines represent links. The intragroup links are common attributes of individuals. The intergroup links are based on contractual relations, as for example in a management by objectives system of control.

A management by objectives system of performance is a form of contractual linkage. Under this system executives are

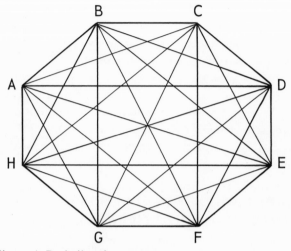

Figure 4. Reticulated, or matrix, organizational structure.

evaluated on the results they achieve as compared with the objectives they have negotiated with their managers. Such objectives have to be realistic and challenging if they are to motivate executives to improve performance. Where there are substantial discrepancies between performance and objective, and no factors out of the control of the executive have intruded, an action plan is negotiated to strengthen areas of weaknesses and improve performance for the coming year. Management by objectives, first discussed by Peter Drucker in *The Practice of Management,* is a system that many people in management are already using in a partial or informal way. All it needs for more effectiveness is some formalization and integration into the overall organizational pattern.

The reticulated, or matrix, organization has many of the advantages of vertical and horizontal organizations, without the disadvantages. In the reticulated organization: (1) The links between persons are based on common attributes. (2) The links between groups are contractual. (3) The links are not highly dependent on emotion, as they are in the vertical organization. (4) Communication is fast, and mobilization to a task is speedy. Links tend to be short, and there are many alternate routes.

In the horizontally organized group, which is the fundamental unit of the reticulated organization, the unit manager plays a role that departs from the classical managerial role. The traditional view is that the manager directs the efforts of workers, checks their results, and uses carrots and sticks (rewards and punishments) to control them.

In contrast, the manager in a horizontal organization is a teacher, a consultant to his own people, a counselor who helps his people evaluate their progress, a communication link between his own small group and the other elements of the organization, and a negotiator of employee performance goals with the employee.

Harland Cleveland, president of the University of Hawaii, who served as a top-level State Department official under Presidents Kennedy and Johnson, believes that public as well as private organizations will require complex structures. He says all managers will be working in large complex systems which he describes as "interlaced webs of tension in which control is loose, power diffused, and centers of decision plural."

Such organizations can combine the advantages of large and small organizational patterns and can accommodate both entrepreneur and hierarch, allowing the advantages of entrepreneurship without undue disturbance of the large company structure.

After a recent trip to China, Joseph Alsop told of the unique bottom-to-top net which rigidly governs that Communist country. One of Mao Tse-tung's key rules is, "Do it yourself, if you possibly can." Chinese planning is from the bottom up instead of from the center down. Central planning experts in Peking deal with consolidated plans, and the central government confines itself to setting the main priorities. This system encourages maximum local effort to meet local needs and greatly simplifies the central planners' task. These are all advantages of giving a high degree of autonomy to local homogeneous units in controlling a vast population.

NEW ORGANIZATIONS IN PRACTICE

Many companies, small and large, are already operating in new patterns. Jim Walter, Textron, Levi Strauss, and Indian Head operate with small corporate staffs and grant varying degrees of decision-making authority to operating managers. In recent years First National City Bank of New York has loosened the traditional rigid structure in banking by giving more authority to operating managers.

Saga Administrative Corporation   Saga Administrative Corporation, with annual sales approaching $200 million, manages food services at more than 450 universities and other institutions. It is an example of a medium-size company that has begun to move in the direction of an entrepreneurial organization. Its goal, as stated by the organizational development staff, is to "encourage an entrepreneurial spirit that will result in personal feelings of power, excitement, fun, and a sense of fulfillment throughout the organization."

Out of a 1968 organizational development program grew the concept of an organization of interlocking teams. Through the vehicle of a functioning team, an individual can make his voice heard in company decision-making processes. And the role of top executives has changed: they act more as coordinators than as order givers or policy makers.

Dow Chemical Company   H. D. Doan, a director and former president of Dow Chemical Company, was the initiator of what Dow calls the business concept. Dow has organized itself around 30 business groups ranging in size from a dozen or so employees to several hundred. Each group makes products that are sold to the same markets or use the same raw materials.

According to C. B. Branch, Dow's president:

Whatever the organizational concept or the targeted activity, it has always been understood in Dow that people are our greatest asset. Other subtle insights which were perceived early and kept alive through the decades are that organization follows ability, that definition is confining, and that motivated freedom results in the acme of productivity. A fundamental requirement for us is an organization that gives meaning to people's lives.[1]

Dow Chemical must be doing something right. It made about 12 percent on total capital in 1972, and its sales, which are now $2.6 billion a year, have grown 10 percent per year for a decade. Now Dow is trying to increase motivation at all levels. For example, in some of the newer plants all employees are salaried; no longer are blue collar workers paid an hourly wage.

Jim Walter Corporation   Jim Walter Corporation is a billion dollar informally run company which reflects the style of its chairman and founder, James W. Walter. Each of its eight profit center units is managed by a vice president, whose role is only partly that of a superior but primarily that of consultant, sounding board, and communication interface for the operating units. Middle managers have complete authority over their operations. Communication flows up from and across all levels of management. Profit center vice presidents make sure their units grow, provide the tools for growth, help in budgeting and planning, and push a little.

[1] Quoted in "Organizing for Fast Change," *Industry Week* (December 11, 1972), pp. 43, 44.

At Jim Walter, down to the level of plant and sales office, managers set their own goals. After goal approval, managers are let alone to try to achieve their goals. Jim Walter looks to its managers for profit and for problem solving. Budgets and financial controls are carefully monitored by profit center and corporate staffs.

Sony Corporation   Despite the high degree of vertical organization in Japanese industry, Sony, the Japanese electronics consumer products company, has been a world pioneer in introducing radical innovations in organization. Shigeru Kobayashi, managing director of Sony, has described the unique features of the organization. For example, at the Atsugi plant there exists an "organization with interconnecting cells." These are vertically and horizontally connected teams, each with two to twenty members. Each team is the smallest possible unit; like a baseball nine or a football eleven, if reduced in size it can no longer function effectively. Each cell not only relates to other teams but also meets weekly to exchange information and decide how to act. The leader is a team member who merely guides the meeting but he is not a power center. Top managers are also not power holders. They are colleagues who help the group of teams in establishing common goals and lead in encouragement and attainment of goals. Group management meetings are held frequently.

What is important to the organizational network at Sony is not command but information. It flows to each cell from above, below, or sideways so that every cell knows what is going on in the other cells. The leader organizes the available information, conducts meetings to allow full discussion, communicates with other teams, encourages the workers, keeps track of progress but does not interfere with his people as they carry out their work, and reviews performance, praising excellence and mentioning weaknesses as items to be corrected.

The production cells in the factory set their own production and quality standards. Experience at Sony shows that once they get this authority, they continually upgrade their own goals so that they can see continuing progress. Standard times and qualities are required only where carrots and sticks are used. As Kobayashi says: "Maybe if we established a standard for the 100-meter dash, nobody would participate in the Olympics. . . . How do you account for the fact that since the days of ancient Greece, new records for the 100-meter dash have been made over and over?"[2]

All employees are free to communicate with all other employees to settle business matters directly in minimum time. Profit and loss is tabulated for each department unit, so that each can evaluate its own function and activity directly. Earning a profit reassures and reinforces the feeling of value, and profit becomes an object of rejoicing instead of hate.

Aerojet-General Corporation   Shortly after Jack Vollbrecht took over in 1971 as president, Aerojet-General developed the concept of management by commitment, a refinement on management by objectives. The result has been (1) a reduction in management manpower, (2) better cost control, (3) reduction of staff needs. A seven-volume *Standard Practices Instructions* has been replaced by a two-page memo. Aerojet's management style is based on results orientation and on stimulation, development, and reward of top performers. There are four organizational principles: (1) The attributes of large and small enterprises are captured with optimum flexibility and speed of action. (2) Each executive does his own planning and organization, and each performs in such a way that his performance can be measured and coordinated. (3) Responsibility and authority are delegated as close to the

[2] *Creative Management.* New York: AMA (1971).

action point as possible. (4) Committees are for communication, not for decisions or action.

THE FUTURE OF THE
NEW ORGANIZATION

Progress toward radically different corporate organization forms is slow but steady. All center on granting increased personal responsibility to individuals at all levels. The change will be welcomed by many of today's managers at both the receiving and giving end. Max Ways has said he is glad that recent college graduates are finally catching on to the tendency to thrust personal responsibility on individuals. "As an editor, I was getting a little weary of young journalists who wanted to be told what to do, and how to do it."

In a survey by Cetron and Overly,[3] 400 American business leaders who read *Innovation* magazine were asked what they think management will be like in 1980. In reply, 61 percent agreed that for the most part "management will be of an internal consultative nature between employees, as opposed to participative or authoritarian," although not all of them agreed on the date. And 59 percent said they do *not* agree that "most companies will have reverted to a tighter, centrally controlled form of management."

A new wind is blowing, and it is a strong wind. Corporate life will not be the same. The security of the vertical organization will go the way of the rigidity of the vertical organization. As Max Ways put it: "Every now and then some young man tells me he has modest career goals. All he wants is a secure, comfortable job. I tell him that not many of those jobs are left. And they will get fewer every year."

[3] Marvin J. Cetron and Don H. Overly, "Disagreeing with the Future," *Technology Review* (March/April 1973), pp. 10–16.

8

PUTTING IT ALL
TOGETHER

THE ENTREPRENEUR is a person who can perform most if not all business functions himself. We generally associate his image with small companies. But large companies, though they are run differently, can use a knowledge of entrepreneurship to advantage in (1) handling new projects, (2) keeping acquired entrepreneurs happy, and (3) adding to the productivity and inner satisfaction of all personnel.

Not all large company activities lend themselves to entrepreneurially oriented individuals. Entrepreneurs can be disruptive in an environment not favorable to their unique type of personality. Yet the business world can no longer get along without large corporations, nor can it get along without entrepreneurs. Large corporations can benefit by proper use of entrepreneurs and entrepreneurial attitudes, just as small companies can benefit by adopting some large company practices.

Bill C. and Herb M., the authors of a new book on entrepreneurship, had lunch with Harold Hierarch, marketing vice president of a $2 billion corporation. "What's the book about?" he asked.

"Our idea was that while large and small companies have to operate in different ways, the way of a small company—the entrepreneurial way—can benefit a large company," said Bill. "Entrepreneurial attitudes, for example, can help in new ventures and can help hold entrepreneurial executives of newly acquired companies.

"In fact, we believe that entrepreneurial attitudes introduced at all levels will benefit the large company. With more widespread education, and generally higher standards of living, workers and executives want more authority and responsibility. They want to do their own thing, be their own man—act as their own boss, so to speak.

"When workers and executives are too tightly controlled and directed, we think they lose interest and become less productive. The better people leave for more rewarding jobs, or they stay and end up with ulcers or a drinking problem. Others spend their time writing memos, playing office politics, and otherwise failing to earn their keep. To avoid this, capabilities should be stretched and jobs should be enriched."

"Oh, come off it," said Harold, "people are just getting lazy, and don't want to work."

"No," said Herb, "they just don't find their work rewarding. We believe that what employees want is a chance to be entrepreneurs of a sort. They want to help set their own goals; they want to be kept informed of their progress through appropriate feedback; and they want to be given as much authority and responsibility as they can handle."

"O.K.," said Harold, "how would that work with my sales force?"

"Give the salesman on the firing line a role in setting his sales quota," Bill answered. "Let him negotiate it with his supervisor. Don't make him too much of a specialist. Always keep him informed on how he's doing: his sales and his contribution to profit. If he falls short of his objectives get him to tell you why he failed and what he can do about the causes under his control. For example, does he need more training of a special kind? In other words, let him help shape his job and set his goals. Help him upgrade his job."

Harold blew up. "You don't realize what a bunch of jerks I have in my crew. Those guys don't know anything. Most of all they don't know quotas. They come out of college thinking they're too good to work. I've always got to be on top of them, tell them what to do every minute; otherwise they'd go running off on some tangent of their own. It won't work."

"Don't you think," asked Herb, "that the salesman, the man on the firing line, should know something about what he can sell and about the potential in his territory? If he doesn't, wouldn't it help to train him to know?"

"Who has the time?" asked Harold. "These guys don't stick around long enough. The turnover is terrific. That's what I keep telling you; they're overgrown kids who don't *want* to work, no matter how hard I drive them. They keep quitting! How can I give responsibility to such irresponsible guys? They aren't entrepreneurs and they never will be!"

Enough said!

Introducing entrepreneurship into the large corporate environment has been likened to teaching an elephant to iceskate. Entrepreneurs have personalities antagonistic to the corporate climate, and many large company business practices discourage entrepreneurship.

The large company can simulate the challenges of small company entrepreneurship, can satisfy the entrepreneurially oriented employee, and can benefit itself by doing so. The hierarch wastes time worrying about *how* to get things done; the entrepreneur *does* things. It is rare for an entrepreneur to be an entrepreneur all the time, and it is rare for anyone in a business management or executive position not to be an entrepreneur at some time.

The qualities that make the entrepreneur are rare indeed; they occur in only a small segment of the population and are not evident unless the business environment is suitable. While entrepreneurs have some characteristics in common, they are hard to identify by tests, psychological or otherwise. They show themselves by their action.

The characteristics of successful and effective entrepreneurial managers in the large corporation include (1) a need to manage people, (2) a need to achieve and have the achievement measured by profits, (3) empathy, (4) ability, (5) willingness to conform to corporate policies. These are not characteristics which we yet know how to instill by schooling or training. Success in school is not related to entrepreneurial success.

An entrepreneur is likely to come from a minority or deprived group and was probably challenged by life from an early age.

The entrepreneurial manager is not a gambler, nor is he overcautious. He carefully measures the risks he undertakes. He is not an egomaniac, not a security seeker, not a crank. He does not fit the mold of the professional manager who wants to do things by the book and measures himself by his effort; instead, the entrepreneur measures himself by profit. He would rather work than play because his fun is his work. And entrepreneurship is as likely to be found in the old as in the young; it does not diminish with age.

To keep entrepreneurs, large corporations have to satisfy their needs to manage and to achieve by granting them responsibility and authority. The proper atmosphere can be created by a marriage of large and small company operational techniques.

There are various ways of introducing entrepreneurship into the large corporation. A classic way is the franchise, which links an independent entrepreneur contractually to a large corporation and gives him the right to make or sell products of the large corporation. In 1971, franchised business accounted for 35 percent of U.S. retail sales.

In recent years, outside of franchising the area of most interest for corporate entrepreneurship has been the new venture. One way of handling the new venture has been through the use of a venture team, a small group of individuals operating in a large company but simulating small company entrepreneurial qualities. Many experiments in the use of venture teams have failed and been abandoned. To be successful, venture teams need full support from the top, patience, dedicated advocates, and a suitable organizational style.

In practice, three main approaches have been taken to the new venture entrepreneurial organization: (1) setting up new ventures of very large potential, with attention focused on a few projects that seem to have the most possibilities; (2) spin-off of small ventures; (3) venture organizations capable of handling any mix of ventures without regard for product line or size. The 3M Company has been notably successful at this, as evidenced by its 40,000 products and its sales that top $2 billion a year.

New venture and new enterprise organizations that were formed in the late sixties tended to change because of the recession that began in 1969 and because of their success in identifying worthwhile projects in the first few years. They turned from finding projects to commercializing those they had found.

How to keep the acquired entrepreneur is a particularly difficult problem. Once an acquisition is carried out, conflict and problems are the rule. But not at U.S. Industries, most of whose 130 or so acquired small companies are managed by the entrepreneurs who started them. The USI management organization can be characterized as fraternal (brother to brother) rather than paternal (father to son). Its unit executives compete against each other, thus minimizing the typical entrepreneur's resistance to authority from a father figure.

Whatever a company's intentions, keeping entrepreneurs happy is not easy. Many acquired entrepreneurs leave or are fired not long after the acquisition. Yet finding ways to keep acquired entrepreneurs happy will become more important as expansion through acquisition becomes a corporate way of life.

The key to corporate entrepreneurship may be the new forms of organization now being created, which make every employee an entrepreneur. In the new organization the large corporation is reshaped into relatively small autonomous teams which are centers of responsibility, authority, and profit, and in which teamwork is the order of the day. Unlike the typical conventional organization, with its highly vertical structure, the new company organization will feature horizontally organized teams laced together into a network, or matrix. The individuals in each team will be held together by common attributes and goals; the teams will be held together by contractual relations—in other words, agreement on common goals and objectives. Management by objectives will prevail. Many companies are already in a transitional phase from the vertical to the reticulated form.

When we talk about introducing entrepreneurship into the large corporation, we are talking about introducing some of the favorable characteristics of the small company into the large company structure. The fact that a company is small does not mean that it is necessarily better. Companies both large and small have unique problems; both can benefit by adopting some of the other's characteristics; both are needed for a vital economy. In a business world in which the small company is a mouse and the large company is an elephant, survival for each may be conditional upon adopting the survival characteristics of the other. For the elephant to adopt some of the survival characteristics of the mouse, he has to learn to walk carefully.

READINGS

ARGYLE, MICHAEL, *The Social Psychology of Work*. London: Penguin, 1972.

BARMASH, ISADORE, *Welcome to Our Conglomerate—You're Fired*. New York: Delacorte Press, 1971.

BERNE, ERIC, *Games People Play*. New York: Grove Press, 1964.

———, *What Do You Say After You Say Hello?* New York: Grove Press, 1972.

CLEVELAND, HARLAND, *The Future Executive: A Guide for Tomorrow's Managers*. New York: Harper & Row, 1972.

COCHRAN, THOMAS C., "Entrepreneurial Behavior and Motivations," *Explorations in Entrepreneurial History* (July 1950).

COLLINS, ORVIS F., DAVID G. MOORE, AND DARAB B. UNWALLA, *The Enterprising Man*. East Lansing: Michigan State University, 1964.

CROCKETT, WILLIAM J., ROBERT E. GAERTNER, AND SAM FARRY, "Humanistic Management in a Fast-Growing Company." In Alfred J. Marrow, ed., *The Failure of Success*. New York: AMA, 1972.

DALES, JOHN H., "Approaches to Entrepreneurial History," *Explorations in Entrepreneurial History* (April 1949).

DESSAUER, JOHN H., *My Years with Xerox*. Garden City, N.Y.: Doubleday, 1971.

DESTLER, C. M., "Entrepreneurial Leadership Among the 'Robber Barons,'" *Journal of Economic History,* Supplement VI (1946).

DURAND, DOUGLAS EUGENE, "Black Entrepreneurship Training," Ph.D. thesis, Washington University, St. Louis, Mo., 1972.

"Entrepreneurs: Luck and Pluck—and a Strong Succession," *Forbes* (September 15, 1967).

146 ENTREPRENEURSHIP AND THE CORPORATION

EPSTEIN, CYNTHIA FUCHS, "Success Among Women," *Chemtech* (January 1973), pp. 8–13.

GOBLE, FRANK, *The Third Force.* New York: Grossman, 1970.

GOODRICH, DAVID L., *Horatio Alger Is Alive and Well and Living in America.* Chicago: Cowles, 1971.

JAY, ANTHONY, *Corporation Man.* New York: Random House, 1971.

JENCKS, CHRISTOPHER, *Inequality.* New York: Basic Books, 1972.

JENKS, LELAND H., "Approaches to Entrepreneurial Personality," *Explorations in Entrepreneurial History* (July 1950).

KNAUTH, OSWALD, *Managerial Enterprise.* New York: Norton, 1948.

LANGER, WALTER C., *The Mind of Adolf Hitler.* New York: Basic Books, 1972.

LEVITT, THEODORE, *The Marketing Mode.* New York: McGraw-Hill, 1969.

LIVINGSTON, J. STERLING, "Myth of the Well-educated Manager," *Harvard Business Review* (January-February 1971), pp. 79–80 ff.; and relevant letters to the editor, May-June 1971, pp. 29 ff.

McCLELLAND, DAVID C., *The Achievement Motive.* New York: Appleton Century Crofts, 1953.

———, *Talent and Society.* Princeton, N.J.: Van Nostrand, 1958.

———, ALFRED L. BALDWIN, URIE BRONFENBRENNER, AND FRED L. STODTBECK, *The Achieving Society.* Princeton, N.J.: Van Nostrand, 1961.

McCLELLAND, DAVID C., "Business Drive and National Achievement," *Harvard Business Review* (July-August 1962), pp. 99–112.

———, *The Roots of Consciousness.* Princeton, N.J.: Van Nostrand, 1964.

———, *Studies in Motivation.* New York: Appleton Century Crofts, 1965.

———, "The Two Faces of Power," unpublished manuscript, September 1968.

———, AND D. WINTER, *Motivating Economic Achievement.* New York: Free Press, 1969.

McGREGOR, DOUGLAS, *The Human Side of Enterprise.* New York: McGraw-Hill, 1960.

McNULTY, HERBERT W., "Entrepreneurship in the Chemical Industry," M.B.A. thesis, New York University, New York, 1967.

MURSTEIN, BERNARD, *Theory and Research in Projective Techniques.* New York: Wiley, 1963.

NEWCOMER, MABEL, *The Big Business Executive: The Factors That Made Him.* New York: Columbia University Press, 1955.

O'TOOLE, JAMES, *Work in America.* Cambridge, Mass.: MIT Press, 1972.

PARK, FORD, "The Technical Strategy of 3M." In *Managing Advanced Technology.* New York: AMA, 1972.

RESEARCH CENTER IN ENTREPRENEURIAL HISTORY, *Change and the Entrepreneur.* Cambridge, Mass.: Harvard University Press, 1949.

RUDIN, SID, "National Motives Predict Psychogenic Death Rate 25 Years Later," *Science* (May 24, 1968), pp. 901–903.

SCHUMPETER, JOSEPH A., *A Theory of Economic Development.* New York: Oxford University Press, 1961.

WARNER, W. LLOYD, AND JAMES ABEGGLEN, *Occupational Mobility in American Business, 1928–1952.* Minneapolis: University of Minnesota Press, 1955.

"Why Entrepreneurs Act the Way They Do," *International Management* (January 1965).

WHYTE, WILLIAM H., JR., *The Organization Man.* Garden City, N.Y.: Doubleday, 1957.

WILSON, COLIN, *New Pathways in Psychology, Maslow and the Post-Freudian Revolution.* London: Gollancz, 1972.

WILSON, JOSEPH, "The Product Nobody Wanted: Xerox." In Sidney Furst and Milton Sherman, eds., *The Strategy of Change for Business Success.* New York: Clarkson N. Potter, 1969.

INDEX

management by perception, 57–58
Mao Tse-tung, 133
matrix organization 131–134
May, Rollo, 73
M.B.A. degree studies, 56–59
Michigan State University, 24–25, 41
Minnesota Mining & Manufacturing Co., 102–106, 143
money, as reward, 53
Monsanto Co., 97
Moog, Inc., 65
Moore, David G., 25–26
Morgan, J. P., 60
motivation, 73–75, 119–121
Murstein, Bernard, 27
Myers, Scott, 20

Naito, Toyoji, 66
National Retail Merchants Association, 71
National Service Industries, 108
needs hierarchy, 17, 32
new products, of 1970s, 97–99
new venture organization, 80–92, 95–96, 124–125, 138
new ventures
    project organization for, 87–88, 94–102
    research and development in, 82–83
    at 3M Company, 103–106
Nicholas, Arthur, 113
Nissan Motor Co., 5

O'Conner, Johnson, 27
Odlum, Floyd, 66
organization, 79–92
    horizontal, 129–131
    matrix, 131–134
    new ventures and, 80–92, 95–96, 124–125, 138
    reticulated, 131–134
    team concept in, 124–125
    vertical, 125–129

Overly, Don H., 138
owner-manager, problem of, 8–9

Pacifico, Carl, 9
parent-child relations, 26, 29–30, 33–34
Pavlov, Ivan, 31
Peard, Michael, 89
perception, management by, 57
performance, ability in, 54–55
Perot, H. Ross, 72
Polaroid-Land cameras, 50
postindustrial society, 21
power, defined, 29–30, 53
profits, vs. stock price, 12–13
psychoanalytical school, views of, 28–30

Radcliffe College, 36
Reagan, Ronald, 67
reputation, importance of, 10–11
Research Center in Entrepreneurial History, 41–42
reticulated organization, 125, 131–134
Rickover, Adm. Hyman, 49–50, 128
Robertson, Wyndham, 35 n.
Rudin, Sid, 30
Russell, Bertrand, 53

safety needs, 16
Saga Administrative Corp., 134
Schumpeter, Joseph A., 23
Scott Paper Co., 99
Securities and Exchange Commission, 36
self-actualization, 17, 73
self-fulfillment needs, 17
Sheehan, Neil, 128
Shopper's Voice, 24
Skinner, B. F., 31–32
small business
    aims and goals of, 2, 8–10
    benefits vs. costs in, 10–11